Keeping the
Central Bank Central

Keeping the
Central Bank Central

U.S. Monetary Policy and
the Banking System

Weir M. Brown
III

Westview Press / Boulder and London

A Westview Special Study

This Westview softcover edition is printed on acid-free paper and bound in softcovers that carry the highest rating of the National Association of State Textbook Administrators, in consultation with the Association of American Publishers and the Book Manufacturers' Institute.

Published in 1987 in the United States of America by Westview Press, Inc.; Frederick A. Praeger, Publisher; 5500 Central Avenue, Boulder, Colorado 80301

Library of Congress Cataloging-in-Publication Data
Brown, Weir M. (Weir Messick), 1914–
   Keeping the central bank central.
   "A Westview special study."
   Bibliography: p.
   Includes index.
   1. Board of Governors of the Federal Reserve
System (U.S.) 2. Monetary policy—United States.
I. Title.
HG2563.B67   1987   332.1'12'0973   87-25416
ISBN 0-8133-7459-6

This book was produced without formal editing by the publisher.

Printed and bound in the United States of America

 The paper used in this publication meets the requirements of the American National Standard for Permanence of Paper for Printed Library Materials Z39.48-1984.

6   5   4   3   2

Contents

Tables and Figures

Preface

In the period just before and after the founding of the Federal Reserve System in 1913, bankers, economists, and legislators were intensely absorbed in discussing how to assure a proper functional relationship between the future central bank and the commercial banking system. Of particular concern were the aims of according the central bank flexible means for extending temporary loans to its member banks at times of economic expansion and for serving as lender of last resort in the event of a financial "panic." To help avoid excesses of credit extension or contraction, the Federal Reserve would also need the control instruments necessary to influence regularly the volume and price of money and credit. The provisions incorporated in the Federal Reserve Act and the techniques that evolved in the germinal period 1913–1923 were felicitous and attracted informed attention in other countries. In the view of one eminent scholar, "In the sense of there being avowed recognition of a complex of public [noncommercial] objectives," that period was "indeed the beginning of the self-conscious, discretionary central banking we know today."[1]

During the sixty-odd years that followed, many changes have occurred to affect one side or the other of the Federal Reserve–banking system relationship. Such diverse phenomena as the negotiable certificate of deposit, interest-rate ceilings, the credit card, the automatic teller machine, electronic check clearing, variable reserve ratios, repurchase agreements, and the Eurodollar market have appeared or disappeared. Changes that have significantly affected the interface between commercial banking operations and the Federal Reserve in its responsibility for conducting a coherent monetary policy have usually called for careful study and suitable adaptation of control methods. In most cases these mutations and the mutual adjustments to them have taken place gradually, without great disorder. Not surprisingly, the two notable exceptions to this pattern of orderly adaptation occurred in the wake of severe conjunctural dislocations: the critical deflationary period of the early 1930s and the prolonged inflationary period of the late 1970s–early 1980s, both of whose domestic manifestations were further aggravated by external shocks and imbalance in international payments positions.

Thus in the financial turmoil of the present decade, the subject of banking and the thrift institutions has commanded more public attention than at any time since the Great Depression. Bank failures and liquidity problems have been uncommonly frequent, due partly to an inflation-induced and generalized discrepancy between loan portfolios incurred earlier at fixed interest rates and the rates now being paid on deposit liabilities, and partly to excessive exposure to vulnerable industrial sectors such as petroleum or agriculture. Besides these solvency-related questions, positions have been taken by some banking industry spokespersons regarding the issues of interstate and nationwide banking firms, ownership by commercial corporations, entry of banks into the fields of insurance or security underwriting, and so on. Public discussion has ranged over diverse relationships, many of them adversarial: banks vs. nonbanks; local vs. interstate depository institutions; the securities industry vs. banking.

Much less attention has been devoted, however, to the current state of the relationship between the banking system and the Federal Reserve in regard to the conduct of national monetary policy. It is to this area—in the fundamentally important field of macroeconomic policy—that this book is addressed. The field is large, and the Federal Reserve Board shares responsibility with other important economic decision-makers for guiding the course of the economy. The book does not undertake to cover the whole subject of macroeconomic policy. What it does seek to examine are two areas that stand squarely at the common border where Fed monetary control meets the banking system. At about the same time that deposit accounts offered at depositories were undergoing marked changes, becoming both more transferable and more interest-bearing, Congressional acts of the early 1980s were lowering or removing reserve requirements from those deposit liabilities of the banking system that were growing most rapidly. Exploration of the implications that these two interfacial changes may have for the conduct of monetary policy constitutes the main object of this book, in the author's hope that it may contribute in modest measure toward maintaining the present effectiveness of the Fed in its crucial position at the center of the U.S. monetary system.

Methods employed in this study are those of fairly simple statistical description and analysis. Given that the object is to examine how the composition and attributes of deposits now compare with those of earlier periods, and similarly to examine the changes over time in the effective levels of required reserves relative to deposits, many of the tables are presented in terms of annual data. Some of these measurements relate to the depository institutions as a group (i.e., including the thrifts), but for reasons of data availability as well as brevity much of the treatment is focused on the commercial banking system. Fortunately, the preponderance of the statistical material needed for analysis was available from published sources. In a few instances in which publication of key Federal Reserve series has been discontinued, the Research and Statistics Division of the Board of Governors kindly provided these data for a few selected dates, which I gratefully acknowledge.

In addition, I was assisted at various stages by conversations with and information supplied by persons at the Board and the several Federal Reserve Banks. I thank them all, and should not fail to mention individually Edward R. Fry, James E. Glassman, Jacqueline A. McDaniel, Mary M. McLaughlin, Ann-Marie Meulendyke, J. Charles Partee, and Daniel L. Rhoads.

The Brookings Institution was very considerate in according me special guest privileges during the course of this study, and the library carrel provided me here was an agreeable base for research and scholarly association. The skill of Mareida Grossman and Deniese A. Young in typing the text and designing the tables was of great assistance.

I owe special thanks to four persons, each of whom read either a part or the whole of the manuscript: Alan S. Blinder, Dennis E. Farley, Donald R. Hodgman, and Alice M. Rivlin. Their written and oral comments were very helpful in confirming, correcting, or redirecting my efforts.

Finally, I thank my wife, Maxine Stewart Brown, for her constructive editorial suggestions at the right moment and my son, Peter D.G. Brown, for his encouragement and interdisciplinary counsel.

Weir M. Brown

Notes

1. R. S. Sayers, "Central Banking," in David L. Sills, ed., *International Encyclopedia of the Social Sciences*, Vol. 2, p. 5 (New York: Macmillan, 1968).

I am by no means an alarmist. I believe that our system, though curious and peculiar, may be worked safely; but if we wish so to work it, we must study it.

—Walter Bagehot, *Lombard Street*, 1873

Introduction

This book examines certain recent changes in commercial banking and in Federal Reserve control practices that, taken together, raise significant implications for the conduct of U.S. monetary policy. In its designated capacity as the nation's central bank, the Federal Reserve System is responsible for formulating and carrying out a monetary policy, or set of policies, designed to facilitate achievement of certain financial conditions and economic goals. These goals are not fixed in number, they vary in relative importance from time to time, and the central bank is not the only official body or private economic agent whose actions influence the course of activity in the economy. Nevertheless, the macroeconomic objectives that are widely accepted as being among the predominant economic concerns of U.S. society ultimately are those of seeking to assure a fairly steady rate of growth in the output of goods and services (i.e., national product in real terms), reasonably stable price and wage levels, high and sustainable levels of employment, and freedom from distortion in the balance of international payments.

The part played by the central bank authorities in pursuing these idealistic and sometimes incompatible objectives is to maintain or seek to create the necessary monetary and financial conditions, both in the present and for the longer term, that will prove to be conducive to the fulfillment of the (largely "real," or physical) economic goals. The means available to the Federal Reserve, as will be discussed at greater length later, consist partly in prescribing rules and conditions (e.g., the discount rate at which it will lend to the banks), and partly in its own direct participation in financial markets. The monetary instruments thus employed exert their influence directly on the commercial banking system and, through that channel, are transmitted throughout the money and capital markets. Therefore, any major change in the nature or operational character of banking will affect the manner and effectiveness of Fed policy actions in accomplishing their desired results. Conversely, any major change in the Federal Reserve's instruments of monetary control that substantially affects the Fed's interface with the money and banking system can equally have consequences in the policy field.

The present study concentrates mainly on two developments affecting this monetary policy relationship between the Federal Reserve and the banks. One of these, the radical restructuring and reduction in the required reserves that depository institutions are obliged to hold against deposits, is extensively analyzed in Chapter 2. That alteration of the reserve instrument, although embodied in the major banking legislation of 1980, has received very little attention in the professional literature. Chapter 1 deals with the mutations over the past ten years in the terms and functional characteristics of the deposit accounts issued by banks. The two subjects of deposits and reserves are obviously mutually related in the framework of the U.S. monetary system. They are of sufficient importance, of themselves, to justify special treatment. Moreover, they should also be seen as very significant—but not the only— examples of the winds of change that are currently affecting the functioning of financial markets, bringing with them at least the potential for future problems.

Chapter 3 gives primary attention to analyzing the consequences stemming from the changed deposit composition and reserve structure for the conduct of Federal Reserve monetary control policy, with special reference to the present nature of open-market operations. It also touches briefly on other evidences of transformation in the financial world with which the Federal Reserve, along with the central banks of other advanced countries, must cope.

1

Bank Deposits:
Transferable and No Rate Ceilings

"What's the use of their having names," the Gnat said, "if they won't answer to them?"

*"No use to **them**," said Alice; "but it's useful to the people that name them, I suppose. If not, why do things have names at all?"*

"I can't say," said the Gnat.

—Lewis Carroll, *Through the Looking-Glass*

Market Turbulence and New Legislation

During the short space of the past ten years, major alterations occurred in the interest rates and other attributes of the deposit accounts offered by commercial banks in the United States. The broad outlines of this history are well known, not simply because the events are recent but because they took place in the well-illuminated arena of competitive struggle among commercial banks, thrift institutions, and mutual fund issuers, during the long, inflation-ridden expansion of the late 1970s and early 1980s, to attract borrowable resources from households and business firms alike. Owing to the familiarity of this development to a wide public, under the broad heading of "deregulation," the treatment here can be comparatively brief. Nevertheless, it is necessary to indicate why the developments of this period appear to be more enduring than those of earlier periods of boom-time disintermediation, and why they affect the monetary relationship of the banks to the Federal Reserve.

Throughout the period since 1933, U.S. banks had been operating under the firm limitations of the Federal Reserve's Regulation Q on the maximum interest rates they were permitted to pay on time and savings deposits.[1] During some past periods when the economy was expanding rapidly and credit demands were strongly pushing up the interest rates paid on short-term market instruments, banks had suffered a loss of deposits, mainly on the part of large holders, to those institutions and instruments not subject to rate ceilings. The resulting tightness of loanable funds at banks, combined with rising interest rates throughout the credit markets, had served in such circumstances to exert a greater or lesser degree of market-generated restraint on the boom, apart from whatever restraints might have been operative from policy actions of the Fed. Extreme examples of such exigencies—which spawned the appellation of "credit crunches"—occurred in 1966 and 1969.[2]

The decade of the 1970s was characterized by a combination of severe distortions in the fields of energy, prices, economic activity, and fiscal operations that put an extraordinary amount of pressure on the volume and terms of credit transactions. These forces were destined to cause successive increases in the deposit-rate ceilings, and ultimately to produce a rapidly-phased removal of them altogether. After the recession of late 1974–1975, the U.S. economy had entered an exceptionally long period of expansion marked by steadily rising employment and income in all sectors. Growing federal deficits added to the upward pressure on resources of a booming private economy that was trying to adapt to the structural changes imposed by the two large increases in the relative price of petroleum. The continued rise in the general price level, after slowing down briefly, began again to accelerate swiftly, and the consumer price index rose by 10 to 13.5 percent in each of the three years 1979–1981.

Concomitantly, the inflationary path of prices was provoking a corresponding movement in interest rates. Lenders and borrowers came to recognize that even the soaring nominal interest rates were, if deflated by a price index, moderate or even negative in real terms. Persistence of registered inflation created expectations of its continuance. The volume of net public and private borrowing combined with the inflationary psychology at the turn of the decade was pushing interest rates to levels that had not prevailed in the U.S. money and capital markets for more than 60 years. Interest on short-term U.S. Treasury bills reached 15 percent, and business firms were borrowing directly on their promissory notes (commercial paper) in the 14–18 percent range.

In this climate, money was being attracted from certificate and other time-deposit accounts of banks to the market instruments whose issuers were not subject to interest-rate ceilings. Moreover, a new instrument was introduced in the large money centers in the form of the money market mutual fund, which proliferated rapidly to become the most successful competitor of the banks, especially for small-denomination accounts. Faced with this deteriorating distortion in the financial markets, the regulatory authorities in 1977–1979 carried out a series of *ad hoc* steps, consisting in raising periodically the interest-rate ceilings within the existing supervisory framework.

This process culminated, however, in a more formal and enduring manner when the Congress, after exhaustive hearings, enacted the Depository Institutions Deregulation and Monetary Control Act of 1980. Title II of this Act provided for a gradual phasing-out and ultimate elimination, within six years, of all restrictions on the maximum rates of interest that may be paid on time and savings deposits by banks and other depository institutions. No change was made in the provision of the amended Federal Reserve Act that prohibits the payment of interest on demand deposits. In addition to stipulating the orderly abandonment of time deposit-rate ceilings, the deregulation portion of this omnibus legislation included various provisions generally broadening certain powers of the depositories, especially those of the thrift institutions.[3]

Many of these other provisions are administrative or are otherwise not relevant to the conduct of Federal Reserve monetary policy, but there is one additional result of the Act that is highly essential to observe. Partly by explicit grant of authority and partly by the breadth of general powers given to the temporary Deregulation Committee entrusted with the liquidation of deposit-rate ceilings, the Congress made no restrictions on the *transfer* privileges attached to bank accounts, either those accounts then existing or those "new categories of accounts" that the committee might create during its life, or that the Federal Reserve Board might later approve.[4] We shall revert to this matter of transferability briefly below, and more extensively in Chapters 2 and 3, for the two attributes of transferability and interest-bearing status of the U.S. banking system's deposit liabilities are closely intertwined, both in monetary theory and in the practical application of the Federal Reserve's monetary policy instruments.

In deciding to require the gradual removal of maximum limits on the interest rates paid on time and savings deposits, the Congress in 1979–1980 was not only acquiescing to the wishes of depositors and the even stronger pressure of the financial intermediaries; it was also adopting the prescriptive viewpoint expressed by certain professional economists and commissions of inquiry in the 1970s. Among the findings of the President's Commission on Financial Structure and Regulation in 1972 was that the original purposes of established ceilings on time and savings deposits were not being served. The commission's report (referred to as the Hunt Report) stated that the drafters of the Banking Act of 1933 had intended that the ceilings, by reducing interest-rate competition among banks, would prevent steep increases of their operating costs and thus would discourage the banks from extending risky, high-yielding loans. This deterrence had not been achieved, it declared. Instead, the voluminous shifting of funds that occurred at times when the ceilings were markedly below other rates in the money markets had by-passed the banks, reduced their ability to serve as intermediaries, affected the liquidity of both banks and business firms, and complicated the Fed's task of controlling money and credit.[5]

In the preamble to the portion of the 1980 act that deregulates the rates on deposits, the Congress stated its view on the damaging effects of interest ceilings in different, less precise, and more florid language than that of the Hunt Report, but the broad conclusions were similar. The provisions of the statute for a gradual but complete elimination of controlled deposit rates constituted a clear Congressional judgment that to allow those rates to be determined by the play of market forces affecting the banks and their deposit creditors would produce results that would both benefit the financial sector itself and contribute to the stability of the economy.

The six-year period prescribed for the progressive freeing of interest rates elapsed at the end of March 1986. Effective on April 1, 1986, the last of the ceilings—that on standard savings account deposits—was removed. Those applying to other types of time and savings deposits had been abolished in separate steps over the period, mainly from late 1982 to January 1986.

Altered Characteristics of Bank Deposits

Having reviewed the market developments and legislative basis affecting the composition of bank deposits, we need to examine in quantitative terms what actual changes have occurred, if any, in the structure of deposits held at banks. We can then analyze, in Chapter 2, the combined effects flowing from the altered deposit liabilities of the banking system and the simultaneous major restructuring of the required reserves against those deposits. It is well to remind the reader that this study does not address itself to any effects these alterations might have on bank competitiveness or profits but to their effects on the relationship between the banking system and the Fed in its conduct of monetary policy.

An available Federal Reserve data series shows deposits outstanding at commercial banks, using the traditional three-way classification: demand, savings, and time deposits. That standard breakdown is satisfactory for many purposes, especially for past years in which each category was fairly homogeneous internally as well as distinguishable from the other two along clear lines. The process of differentiation within categories began slowly, notably with the evolution of the large-denomination (over $100,000) certificate of deposit, in the early 1960s, to a new life as a negotiable market instrument. But the pace accelerated in the 1970s, and the banking system now displays:

1. two classes of interest-bearing savings deposit: the standard passbook account and the money market deposit account, the latter with liberal, if limited, transfer privileges;

TABLE 1.1
Deposit liabilities outstanding at all commercial banks, by type of deposit, 1977-1986[1]/ (billions of dollars)

	1977	1979	1981	1983	1984	1985	1986
Interest-bearing							
Money mkt. deposit acct.	--	--	--	217.3	242.6	317.7	361.9
Super NOW	--	--	--	25.6	31.5	40.3]	142.8
NOW and ATS	n.a.	n.a.	n.a.	66.6	68.7	76.8]	
Savings deposits	215.4	218.8	218.0	138.8	126.4	124.0	135.8
Small denom. time dep.	182.0	225.0	343.9	360.5	417.7	442.8	445.3
Large denom. time dep.	131.2	199.2	293.2	287.7	312.8	317.0	346.4
Total, interest-bearing	528.6	643.0	855.1	1,096.5	1,199.7	1,318.6	1,432.2
Not interest-bearing							
Demand deposits	324.9	370.0	360.8	348.1	339.3	358.3	401.4
TOTAL, all deposits	853.5	1,013.0	1,215.9	1,444.6	1,539.0	1,676.9	1,833.6
Percent of total bearing interest	61.9%	63.5%	70.3%	75.9%	78.0%	78.6%	78.1%

Sources: Calculated from data in monthly Bulletin and other Federal Reserve Board publications.

Notes: 1. Figures given pertain to last Wednesday of August for recent years (July for 1977-1981).

n.a. = not available

2. three classes of "transaction" accounts: the traditional demand deposit with full transfer powers and no interest return; the "checkable" and interest-bearing NOW account (for deposits of households and non-profit organizations only); and the interest-bearing ATS account linked for automatic transfer to a checking account. For a short time prior to and after the 1980 deregulation, NOW and ATS had been labeled as savings accounts;

3. two size-classes of time deposits, the dividing point between the small and large being $100,000. Both sizes exist in certificate and statement-account form, though the CD form predominates; the large CD is negotiable.

Owing to these complexities, it is preferable to depart from the simple demand/savings/time breakdown in order to show comparative growth paths of individual deposit types. Table 1.1 presents bank deposits outstanding, distributed by separate class but grouped as to those that are interest-bearing and those not. In 1977, the interest-earning group, comprising three types of time and savings deposits, totaled $529 billion and represented 62 percent of all commercial bank deposits. In the subsequent years, the proportion of deposits bearing interest continued to rise, reaching almost 79 percent in 1985, against 62 percent in 1977. The most rapid increase came, not unexpectedly, in the period 1980 through 1983, which included the extension of authorization for NOW and ATS accounts to a nationwide scope, as well as the appearance of money market deposit accounts (MMDA).

Demand deposit balances had been growing less rapidly than time (including savings) deposits, and hence falling slowly as a percentage of total deposits, since the early 1960s. Numerous factors were at work to raise the volume of time deposits and to promote or permit a slower growth of demand accounts. There is little doubt, however, that the introduction of innovative types of interest-earning accounts with enlarged transfer terms in the early 1980s served not merely to retard the drain of time-deposit resources from the banking system toward the mutual funds but, after a time, to restore the growth. Note that in 1977 the standard savings account had the largest balances in the time and savings group. By 1984, savings deposits had declined about 40 percent and demand balances were still not much above the 1977 level, while the newer or modified accounts had accounted for the bulk of the growth.

Given that new types of interest-bearing bank accounts were introduced and that the volume of such balances was increasing more rapidly than the other types, it could be expected that the banks' annual volume of interest payments on deposits would rise substantially as shown below:

	1977	1979	1981	1983	1985
Total deposits	100.0	118.7	142.5	169.3	196.5
Total interest paid on deposits	100.0	185.3	358.7	309.7	333.0

The three new deposit types, MMDA, NOW, and ATS, are estimated to account for 29 percent of total interest payments in August 1985 and 33 percent in August 1986.

The differences between deposit classes with regard to the comparative movements of their interest rates are apparent in Table 1.2. Inflation and the rather gradual pace at which rate ceilings were being removed largely explain the wide dispersion (between controlled and uncontrolled interest levels) at commercial banks during 1980–82. As inflation was brought progressively under control, large CDs again exhibited the most sensitivity. Disinflation, slower growth of the economy, and ceiling removal were gradually reflected in a lowering in all deposit rates. In addition, these factors lately produced a marked convergence, in absolute terms, with August 1986 showing a range of only 1.0 percentage points among the five average interest rates. This high a degree of convergence is not likely to continue. It does seem to imply that the depository market was, at that month in mid-1986, evaluating the differing bundles of utilities embodied in the respective deposit instruments as being roughly equivalent. A change in economic growth rates or in inflationary pressures, for example, could affect the interest-rate spreads as well as the relative volumes of the different deposits outstanding.

The addition of new types of bank deposit that are interest-bearing and the rise (or fall) in the rate of return on those accounts have, in themselves, some implications for U.S. monetary policy. For example, economists have for a long time recognized that the demand for narrowly-defined "money" in an economy (sometimes expressed as the willingness to hold cash balances) is influenced by various factors, among which is the amount of income foregone by owning cash rather than income-producing assets. Thus the size of the differential between the return on holding an interest-earning deposit and the return on a no-interest checking account or currency can affect the comparative growth of these respective variables. And since some of these monetary entities are considered by the central bank to be motive forces in propelling economic activity and income, while other entities are considered of little relevance to that process, the two groups are likely to be treated differently by the authorities in the devising and execution of monetary policy.

While the innovation in bank deposits has been characterized by changes in the field of interest payment, the other major characteristic is the heightened

TABLE 1.2
Average interest rates on deposit liabilities, by type of deposit, and weighted-average composite rates, at all commercial banks, 1977–1986 (at mid-year month; in percent)

	1977	1979	1981	1983	1984	1985	1986
Interest-bearing							
1. Money mkt. deposit acct.	--	--	--	8.57	9.32	6.75	5.48
2. Super NOW	--	--	--	7.47	7.65	6.06 }	5.25
3. NOW and ATS	n.a.	n.a.	n.a.	5.25	5.25	5.25	5.34
4. Savings deposits	4.91	5.15	5.21	5.50	5.50	5.50	6.25
5. Small denom. time dep.	6.35	7.25	12.97	10.08	11.22	8.10	5.92
6. Large denom. time dep.	5.91	10.11	17.96	9.77	11.47	7.81	
7. Total, interest-bearing[1]	5.65	7.42	12.70	8.77	9.86	7.23	5.79
Not interest-bearing							
8. Demand deposits	.0	.0	.0	.0	.0	.0	.0
9. Total, all deposits[1]	3.50	4.71	8.93	6.65	7.69	5.69	4.52
Memo item:							
Average rate paid for interest-bearing deposits[2]	5.72	8.69	13.42	9.32	9.92	8.55	n.a.

Sources: Calculated from deposit figures in Table 1.1 and interest-rate data on rates in effect at Fed survey data (monthly since 1983, quarterly in prior years). Lines 7 and 9 are weighted averages for interest-bearing and total deposits, respectively.

Notes: 1. Weighted average. 2. From annual Bulletin articles on bank profitability. The series quoted is calculated by the Board in manner described in Bulletin, Sept. 1979, p. 704.

n.a. = not available

degree of liquidity and transferability that deposits have acquired. Up to the late 1970s, the only type of account at commercial banks that was transferable by means of a check drawn in favor of a third party was the standard demand or "checking" account,[6] which constituted 38 percent of total bank deposits. By 1983, three additional transferable accounts (MMDA, NOW, and ATS) had emerged[7]; and even though there had been a great increase in the volume of time certificate accounts, the quantity of checkable deposits had risen from 38 percent of total deposits in 1977 to 46 percent in 1983 and 49 percent in 1986.

Although the check-drawing feature is the clearest criterion of deposit transferability, other methods for making payments from a deposit balance have been incorporated in some bank accounts. For example, the MMDA may allow up to six transfers to third parties per month, of which three may be by check; shifts to other accounts of the holder in the same bank; and unlimited withdrawals by mail, by messenger, or in person. There is no dollar limit on transfers. In addition, original requirements that NOW and MMDA holders must maintain minimum average balances of $2,500 have been reduced and are now eliminated. A change producing increased *liquidity* of time deposits, as contrasted with transferability, is that the 1980 statute lowered the maximum waiting period for withdrawal of a time deposit from 14 days after the date of deposit to seven days.

On closer inspection, it becomes clear that the several types of deposit liability of the banking system differ somewhat from one another in respect of the degrees or forms of both liquidity and transferability that they embrace. Although these elements are not precisely quantifiable, especially in com-bination, it is nevertheless useful to construct a table listing the six main categories of bank deposit roughly according to the forms of liquidity and transfer properties they possess (Table 1.3). Displaying the banking system's deposit liabilities in this manner evokes two observations. First, the listing exhibits procedural differences between deposit types as to whether they can be augmented or withdrawn by the holder fractionally, and whether the holder's access is by withdrawal, redemption, or market sale; whether withdrawal or liquidation is paid at par on demand or requires loss of interest; whether a transfer to a third party is made by check or other draft directly or involves an intermediate transaction, etc. Second, despite the many different combinations of terms among the several types of deposit, the general level of effective liquidity and transferability is very high. This high degree of accessibility is paralleled, as noted earlier, by the fact that at present more than three quarters of total bank deposits are also interest-bearing. Indeed, it is this *combining* of transferability, liquidity, and income that is new and requires analysis.

The extent to which the various types of bank deposits are *functionally* diverse or similar is a question that is never new, but always relevant. Not

TABLE 1.3
Classification of deposits at commercial banks according to degrees and
forms of liquidity and transferability (billions of dollars)

Type of account	1977		1986	
	Amount	% of total	Amount	% of total
Liquid and transferable	$324.9	38.1%	$906.1	49.4%
Demand deposit	324.9	38.1	401.4	21.9
NOW and ATS	--	--	142.8	7.8
MMDA	--	--	361.9	19.7
Liquid but not checkable				
Savings account	215.4	25.2	135.8	7.4
Transferable by sale in secondary market 1/				
Large denomination CD2/	131.2	15.4	346.4	18.9
Liquid by redemption, with penalty				
Small denomination CD3/	182.0	21.3	445.3	24.3
	853.5	100.0	1,833.6	100.0

Sources: Regulation D and other F.R. Board publications, and preceding
          tables.

Notes: 1. Holder can sell whole principal in secondary market but not
          fractional amount. 2. Negotiable CD can be liquidated by
          individual holder, but it remains a liability of issuing bank
          until maturity. 3. Holder can redeem from issuer the whole or
          part of principal before maturity, but forfeits portion of
          interest, according to specified scale.

new, because monetary economists and central bankers often make (and
revise) classifications that delineate either a sharp or a vague distinction
between what constitutes money and what is regarded as "near-monies."
Heretofore, the concept of money as a means of payment was held by
many to embrace only those assets instantly available for transactional
purposes, universally negotiable without discount, and earning no explicit

income. When applied in the context of the U.S. monetary system until recently, this appeared to mean that the demand deposit was the only bank account to qualify as a component of the money stock.[8] Developments have now placed this in doubt.

As banking practices evolve, this question of definition and interpretation remains relevant to the task of conceptualizing and implementing a macroeconomic policy by the central bank. In carrying out its short- and long-term policy responsibilities mentioned in the opening paragraphs, the Federal Reserve is obliged to concern itself with the terms and attributes of the deposit aggregates—as well as all liabilities of the banking system—for two basic reasons. First, in order to determine which of them, if any, qualify as forms of "money" whose behavior should be carefully monitored and, to the extent necessary, stimulated or restrained: i.e., in the choice of the so-called "targets" to be tracked. A second relevant point of Fed concern is to determine how and to what degree the respective target or targets chosen should be affected by, or exposed to, the Fed's major instruments of monetary-control policy.[9]

The wisdom with which those decisions are reached can make a significant contribution to maintaining a comprehensive, effective interface between the banking system and the Federal Reserve: that is, to the goal of keeping the central bank central in the monetary system.

In Chapters 2 and 3, we shall examine how the changed set of bank deposits is now affected by a restructured set of required reserves; and what further implications both sorts of change hold for the overall conduct of monetary policy.

Notes

1. Authority to establish ceiling rates for Federal Reserve member banks was embodied in the Banking Act of 1933, and similar authority was given to the bodies governing other depository institutions.

2. In a critical period, the credit stringency tended to be particularly severe with regard to long-term mortgages at fixed rates. This posed a policy problem for government as to whether to subsidize residential housing or to allow market forces to determine the mortgage rates and volume.

3. For further background on the deposit-rate controls and the 1980 legislation, see Young, pp. 155–59; Mayer *et al.*, Ch. 8; Cargill and Garcia, Ch. 5; Federal Reserve Bank of Chicago.

4. Title III of the Act specifically extended to all banks the authority for NOW (negotiable order of withdrawal) accounts and ATS (automatic transfer service) accounts. Title I, the Monetary Control portion of the omnibus statute, designates NOW and ATS, along with share draft accounts at thrifts, as "transaction accounts" within the meaning of the Act, and gives the Federal Reserve Board of Governors authority to determine that other accounts are transaction accounts if they "may

be used . . . directly or indirectly . . . for payments or transfers to third persons or others." P.L. 96–221, 96th Cong., Title I, Sec. 103(b), (1).

5. President's Commission, pp. 23–29, and Mayer *et al.*, pp. 197–213. A different interpretation of this history is presented by Wojnilower's "defense of credit crunches."

6. The NOW account had been permitted only in certain New England states in the 1970s. The 1980 legislation referred to above granted banks nationwide the authority to establish NOW accounts, beginning January 1981.

7. The ATS and NOW are defined, by law, as "transaction" accounts and, as such, are subject to the same treatment under the reserve requirements as demand deposits. Under Fed money supply definitions, they are included in M1. MMDAs, by contrast, are treated for reserve purposes with the time/savings group; and are listed in the M2 money supply. These matters will be analyzed further in Chap. 2.

8. Henderson, pp. 11–35; Samuelson, pp. 262–65.

9. *Cf.* Sayers, Chapter 1; Young, pp. 28–29, 52–53.

2

Required Reserves:
Restructured and Reduced

The Great Wall of China was finished off at its northernmost corner . . . in two sections of piecemeal construction. . . . But after the junction the groups of workers were transferred to begin building again in quite different neighbourhoods. Naturally in this way many great gaps were left. . . . In fact, it is said that there are gaps which never have been filled. . . .

Not only cannot such a wall protect, but . . . it is in perpetual danger. These blocks . . . could easily be pulled down again and again by the nomads, especially as these tribes . . . kept changing their encampments . . . like locusts, and so perhaps had a better general view . . . than we, the builders.

—Franz Kafka, *The Great Wall of China*

Public attention to the changing relationship between U.S. commercial banks and the public monetary authorities has concentrated largely on the successive steps taken, as traced above, regarding the determination of interest rates and other terms applied by banks to the funds they borrow from depositors. Those steps culminated in a major piece of banking legislation—one portion of the Depository Institutions Deregulation and Monetary Control Act of 1980—which undertook to legitimize a path that commercial banks and thrifts could follow, freed of interest-rate ceilings. The present chapter deals with the other portion of this omnibus statute that introduced several changes pertaining to the mandatory reserve requirements administered by the Board of Governors of the Federal Reserve System. Falling under the apt title of "monetary control," these provisions have a potential for affecting significantly the conduct of U.S. monetary policy. We shall examine these amendments to the required-reserve system, and their implications; but first, a summary of the reserve situation that preceded the change.

As concerns the obligation for banking institutions to maintain reserves against their depository liabilities, the U.S. banking system prior to 1980 had exhibited several main characteristics. First, there existed a uniform, clearly-defined set of rules mandated by the Board of Governors and applicable to banks that were members of the Federal Reserve System; and side-by-side with the Fed's regime for member banks were the various regimes promulgated by the several state governments for other banks. Second, not only were the state rules diverse, across states, in their definition and severity for the individual bank, they also played a different macroeconomic role from that of the Federal Reserve type, especially at times of cyclical peaks and troughs. Third, the relative strictness (from the standpoint of the individual bank) of the FRB requirements as compared with those of the states was, in the later years, provoking a steady flow of membership withdrawals—except for the nationally-chartered institutions obliged to belong to the System. This latter problem of membership had a growing potential for weakening the effectiveness of the Board's monetary management.

From its beginning, the Federal Reserve System had embodied the principle that its member commercial banks were obliged to set aside a prescribed amount of money as "required reserves." These reserves are not only calculated as a certain specified percentage of a given bank's deposits in each of several categories, but are often spoken of as reserve's "against deposits." The form in which reserves could legally be held vacillated somewhat in the earlier years between cash in the bank's own vault and an account balance at the regional Federal Reserve Bank. Since 1960, a bank could fulfill its reserve requirement by any combination of vault cash and its balance at the Reserve Bank. The requirement is stated in terms of maintaining the given level *on average* over a fourteen-day maintenance period.

Broadly speaking, the obligation of setting aside, or reserving, a portion of bank funds was adopted by the monetary authorities (and accepted to varying degrees in the banking industry) in a certain recognition of the principle that commercial banking can legitimately be practiced on the basis of a current assets/current liabilities ratio far below 100/100. Given certain assumptions about stable macroeconomic conditions, articulated financial markets, and the existence of institutional safeguards, the fractional reserve principle functions well for the banking system as a whole as well as for the individual firm. If the volumes of economic activity and bank credit in the economy are expanding, the money lent enters the expenditure stream and raises the aggregate level of bank deposits. An obligation requiring the maintenance of a specified ratio between deposits and the reserve balances held causes the reserves of the banking system as a whole to rise as a function of total deposits (or, at least, of reservable deposits).[1] The volume of lendable funds, therefore, does not rise to the full extent of the deposit increase, and the reserve requirement thus acts as a mild brake on credit expansion.

In fixing the respective ranges within which reserve ratios for the several categories of deposits could be set by the Board of Governors, the Federal Reserve Act and the Board's application of it presumably reflected the prevailing practice and banking theory that deposit liabilities of different liquidities carried different degrees of risk. Since, in banking experience, the liquidity and volatility risk had commonly been associated with maturity designations, the Fed's requirements on members differentiated between demand, saving, and time deposits. In the period just preceding the 1980 legislation, for instance, the percentage to be reserved for time deposits at member banks amounted to one to six percent, varying inversely with the maturity and directly with the volume. A member's demand deposits, on the other hand, called for reserves from 7 to 16.25 percent, depending on the total volume outstanding.[2]

It is essential to be clear as to the functional or operational role played in the economy by required bank reserves of the kind embodied in the Federal Reserve System. The word "reserve" is to a degree misleading, unless one recognizes that it is a term of art in the Federal Reserve System that carries a connotation different from that of common accounting parlance. For the individual banking firm, the cash that is set aside to fulfill the requirement does not constitute either a general or a specific contingency reserve that can be drawn upon without limit to meet, for example, major fluctuations in its deposit level or a prolonged upswing in its loan demand. For such purposes, the bank has several sources at option (e.g., issuing additional certificates or borrowing from the Fed discount window), but the specified amount of its reserve is not a financial resource accessible to the member for withdrawal unless its quantity of reservable deposits decreases. Nor is the banking firm's required reserve balance a form of insurance affording protection to individual depositors (or the bank itself) in the event of a large-scale "run" of withdrawals.[3] To deal with that risk, it was necessary to establish the Federal Deposit Insurance Corporation (FDIC) in the 1930s. This must not, however, be misunderstood to mean that a bank's reserve *account* is either idle or provides no benefit to the bank itself. Quite the contrary. The individual bank or thrift institution's obligation, during the fourteen-day reserve "maintenance period," is to maintain a minimum *average* balance of a specified level based on its deposit liabilities. While fulfilling this obligation, the typical bank will daily have various payments or receipts charged or credited to its reserve account balance at its regional Reserve Bank.

Nevertheless, the requirement for banks to maintain an impounded cash set-aside is, above all, an instrument of monetary control and, in turn, of overall demand management. Indeed, it is the macroeconomic role played by the aggregate volume of reserves of the banking system that explains the primary purpose of the reserve requirement, rather than its effect on, or usefulness to, the individual bank. The relationship of aggregate reserves to other major variables and the manner in which the required-reserve tool relates to other monetary instruments of the Federal Reserve System are extensively covered in the literature.[4] For the present purposes, it is important to recall two functions relevant to the goals of monetary control that reserves perform. One obvious option available to the monetary authorities is the possibility of raising or lowering the percentage ratios in force, thus decreasing or increasing the volume of non-borrowed reserves that the banking system can use to grant credit and increase deposits. This type of action lies within the sole responsibility of the Board of Governors, can be applied promptly, acts directly on the reserve base rather than through other transactions (as open market operations do), and affects all banks rather uniformly, in percentage and in timing. In fact, its force is so rigorous and rapid on member bank asset-dispositions that it is the least-employed of the Board's possible actions.

The second service performed by the required reserves is a continuing rather than discretionary one: that of constituting a monetary aggregate of significant mass to interact with other policy instruments and market developments. When, for example, the Fed's Open Market Account sells a quantity of federal government securities, the purchasers' banks pay for them by drawing a check to the Fed from their reserve holdings, thereby either using any cash they may hold excess to requirements or necessitating a replenishment of the required balance. In the absence of the legal obligation to maintain a specified percentage, the banking community would be free to lower its relative cash holdings, and the objective of credit tightening that motivated the open market sale would be offset. It is this attribute of the required reserve stock that is highly valued in Federal Reserve circles and has caused required reserves to be referred to commonly in the trade as the fulcrum on which the lever of open market transactions exerts its force.

Non-member Banks and Thrifts

In 1980, when the Federal Reserve Board's jurisdiction over banking institutions' reserves was still limited to members of its System, its scope comprised about 38 percent of all U.S. commercial banks. Those members accounted, however, for about 71 percent of all commercial bank deposits. The nearly 9,000 banks that had elected not to become members were subject to whatever rules concerning reserve funds were imposed by governments of the states in which they were chartered. The same was true of mutual savings banks and other thrift institutions whose reserve obligations were to be embraced by the new legislation. Although the states' provisions showed a considerable heterogeneity as to types of deposit covered, reserve ratios, and rigor of enforcement, the prevailing practice was to stipulate that some percentage of deposit liabilities be held as vault cash, governmental securities, or credit balances at correspondent banks.

It should be noted that the two systems of required reserves (that of the Federal Reserve Act and those of the states) differed significantly in their operational impact, despite their superficial similarity. Whereas the FRB's requirements resulted in impounded balances insulated from current financial activity, the state-regulated depositories fulfilled their reserve obligations largely through investment in asset-holdings that were negotiable liabilities of other entities *within* the economy: balances with correspondent commercial banks, and Federal or local government securities.[5] Non-member institutions were thus free to shift and to alter the mix of their reserve holdings among a more diverse and partly income-producing group of assets. Moreover, most states permitted a bank to count as reserves the checks owed to it but still in process of collection.

At the aggregate level, the two different concepts of reserves existed side by side, and during periods of economic stability they fraternized fairly well. The potentially troublesome element of reserve double-counting involved in the correspondent-bank relationship was not felt at times of slack. When minor increases or decreases in the amount of credit were desired by the Board, open market operations could be expected ultimately to affect all banks, albeit unevenly and with lags. But the non-member depositories' reserves formed no part of the "fulcrum" of sterilized reserves at any given date; and steady shrinkage in the number of member banks was progressively eroding the effective size of that fulcrum, relative to the mounting total-deposits component in the money supply over time. During periods of marked tightness in the whole economy, moreover, the dual reserve systems functioned less smoothly. Even the larger correspondent banks might at such times be having difficulty meeting their own reserve requirements at their Reserve Bank and could not extend further credits to their client banks. A member's borrowing request to the Reserve Bank could, in principle, include something toward meeting a client bank's need, but a request involving a pass-through of this sort required express approval of the Board of Governors.

Monetary Control Legislation

The monetary control portion (Title I) of the Depository Institutions Deregulation and Monetary Control Act of 1980 wrought major changes in the respective roles of state governments and of Federal authorities—the latter including the Congress and especially the Federal Reserve System. In addition, the legislation incorporated a few changes in approach to the subject of required reserves that altered the manner in which both the

Board and the depository institutions treat different categories of deposits. Some of these provisions represent the desire to correct earlier demonstrable weaknesses of banking industry structure, while others reflect the fluctuating currents of economic and monetary theory. In the process, the relationship of the Federal Reserve with the banks and other depositories has been modified, with possible consequences for the conduct of monetary policy by the central bank.

The principal substantive alterations introduced by the Monetary Control Act (MCA) are as follows:

1. The Federal Reserve Board's previous jurisdiction over the required reserve holdings of its member banks was extended to all U.S. depository institutions.[6] For the same group of financial institutions, the right of access to the discount window of the Reserve Banks was also accorded.

2. New ranges of permissible reserve ratios, within which the Board is authorized to fix the respective percentages of reserves required for different classes of deposits, were established for normal operations. Collectively, these substantially lowered the total reserves/deposits ratio.[7]

3. The designation of deposits regarded as subject to reserve requirements was changed, so as to embrace only "transaction deposits" (demand and other checkable accounts) and certain "nonpersonal" time deposits (accounts owned by other than natural persons). Transaction deposits were assigned a somewhat lowered range of reserve ratio. Short-term time deposits were made reservable for "nonpersonal" accounts; but all other time and saving deposits are free of reserves.

The legislative decision to bring various types of depository institutions under one rule-making authority for reserve requirements was a response, in varying degrees, to several perceived problems. In a geographical sense, financial markets have increasingly extended beyond national boundaries, and *a fortiori* certainly are not co-terminous with U.S. state borders. The 50 different sets of state rules for bank reserves have constituted a political obstacle to achieving either greater homogeneity of competitive conditions among banking firms, on one hand, or more uniform control over the economy's money supply, on the other. Moreover, as earlier noted, the greater laxity of reserve rules issued by state governments had been sufficiently enticing to cause a steady fall in Federal Reserve membership. This decline was progressively weakening the Fed's reserve instrument (comprising both the *stock* of accumulated required reserves and *ad hoc* variations in the prevailing required *ratios*) as a policy tool. From the early 1960s to 1980, the percentage share of member banks in the adjusted demand and time deposits of all commercial banks had declined from about 83 to 71 percent.[8]

A very precipitous further drop was feared in 1980 to be imminent. In addition, the inflation-induced rise in nominal interest rates and in competition among financial firms for borrowable funds in the late 1970s was producing a growth of accounts at other financial institutions that resembled the reserve-subject accounts of commercial banks themselves.

Evaluating the effects of the MCA on the membership-drain problem can be approached in various ways. Data showing the number of insured commercial banks at mid-year are broken down between members and non-members. The decline in member banks mentioned in the preceding paragraph reached its low point in 1980, both in absolute numbers and as a share of all insured commercial banks. From 1980 to 1986, the percentage of members rose from 37.6 to 42.0 (preliminary) percent, a level last reached in 1971. The rise in System membership was roughly matched by a decreased number of non-member banks. While the relative share of member banks in total commercial bank deposits also has begun to recover, the process has been much slower and later. In this series, the member-bank share continued to decline slowly to its low point in 1983, at 70.7 percent of all commercial bank deposits. By mid-1986, this share had recovered only to 71.9 (preliminary) percent (Table 2.1).

One must recognize that the MCA of 1980 directed that all commercial banks (and other designated depositories) be brought under the same regime as the member banks with regard to reserve requirements as well as access to the Reserve Bank lending facilities and technical services. These provisions, by extending to all depository institutions the main functional obligations and rights heretofore applying to members, gave them roughly equivalent exposure to the Fed instruments of monetary-control policy. In effect, therefore, this action virtually rendered moot the question of membership, in the sense of control previously connoted by that term.[9] From that point on, the former concern over *membership* had been dealt with by a legislative act of uniform institutional coverage. Though the MCA sought to settle the chronic institutional problem, it created a new difficulty for monetary control policy by drastically re-defining the deposits subject to reserve requirements at *all* institutions, as will appear later in this chapter.

If other depositories were to be brought under the Federal Reserve's regime on required reserves, it was logical to make them eligible also to borrow from the Fed's discount facility. Obliging a nonmember commercial bank to conform to the FRB requirement for setting aside money in its vaults or at the Reserve Bank meant that almost certainly it would reduce its balance with a correspondent bank, not because its new set-aside was a resource it could draw upon—we have seen that it is not—but because the bank could not afford to maintain both types of "reserve." The MCA recognized the desirability of giving to all depositories covered by the reserve provisions the same right of access to the Federal Reserve discount facility

TABLE 2.1
Number of Federal Reserve member banks, and their total deposits, relative to all insured commercial banks, 1974-1986

End of Month	Number of banks				Volume of deposits (billions of dollars)			
	All commercial banks	FRS member banks		Non-members	All commercial banks	FRS member banks		Non-members
		Number	Percent of total			Number	Percent of total	
Dec. 1974	14,216	5,780	40.7	8,436	741.6	575.8	77.6	165.8
Sept 1978	14,390	5,594	38.9	8,796	960.7	701.3	73.0	259.4
June 1980	14,395	5,407	37.6	8,988	1,101.0	785.7	71.4	315.3
June 1981	14,443	5,472	37.9	8,971	1,210.7	861.7	71.2	349.0
June 1982	14,413	5,538	38.4	8,875	1,291.8	916.0	70.9	375.8
June 1983	14,465	5,724	39.6	8,741	1,436.7	1,016.3	70.7	420.5
June 1984	14,373	5,825	40.5	8,548	1,523.6	1,078.9	70.8	444.7
June 1985	14,491	6,054	41.8	8,437	1,656.6	1,179.1	71.2	477.5
June 1986p	14,186	5,954	42.0	8,232	1,805.9	1,298.4	71.9	507.5

Source: Computed from tables in the Annual Report of the Board of Governors of the Federal Reserve System for the years covered.

Note: p = preliminary

as a source of borrowing, as well as the right to buy the check-clearing, wire-transfer, and other Fed services. Another section of MCA Title I authorizes the Federal Reserve to obtain from depository institutions "such reports of . . . liabilities and assets as the Board may determine to be necessary or desirable" for discharging its monetary control responsibilities. Taken together, these provisions enable the Board to possess individual and aggregate information on the amounts of credit, deposit liabilities, and reserves (both borrowed and nonborrowed) of the depository institutions embraced by the Act. At the same time, however, the statute did not include one competitive institution, and it substantially lowered the reserve coverage of the liabilities of the commercial banks themselves.

Recalling the swift growth of money market funds in the late 1970s and the large amount of disintermediation caused by that development, one cannot avoid asking why the list of types of depository institution now covered fails to include the money market funds. The dollar volume of such fund accounts ranged as high as 7 to 9 percent of M2 (in which they are classified by the Fed) in the years just before and following passage of the Act. Complaints had been vociferous from the banking and thrift industries, especially by the small to medium-size firms, about the drainage of deposits to these new accounts and their relative freedom from both regulation and deposit insurance. The omission of the money funds seems to be explained by several factors. The Fed and the Congress had already embarked, prior to the MCA's passage, on a different approach to the disintermediation problem—and one widely urged by the banks themselves—in the form of successive relaxations of the Regulation Q ceilings on interest payments. Moreover, the investment-industry sponsors of the money market funds lobbied vigorously about real and purported differences between their operations and accounts and those of the banks. Besides, the largest banks were marketing money funds of their own. As a result, the compromise that emerged appears to be that the money market funds were omitted from the Act's purview; and the legislation defined time deposits in a manner which would later enable the "money market deposit accounts" (MMDAs)—when authorized by the Garn–St. Germain Depository Institutions Act of 1982—to be classified as "savings deposits subject to time deposit reserve requirements."[10]

A brief word is needed on the status of state government regulations on bank reserves. The MCA, though extending the Federal Reserve's jurisdiction over reserve requirements to all depositories, is silent about the pre-existing rules of the states. According to informal information available to the Board's legal division, the situation varies across states. Some have taken action announcing that adherence to the Board's requirements is accepted as fulfilling their own; some have rescinded their reserve rules; and some are known to have taken no position. Although some nominal duplication no doubt exists, the *de facto* situation is that all parties appear to be accepting the Board's control as binding, without major difficulty. (This may have been facilitated by the graduality of the "phase-in" of the new institutions, to be mentioned later.)

The following paragraphs will compare the reserve-subject deposits and the applicable reserve ratios, under the new legislation, with the corresponding previous requirements. After that, the changes in *effective* magnitudes that have resulted from applying the new rules will be presented and analyzed.

The New Reserve Requirements

Before entry into force of the Monetary Control Act in 1980, the Federal Reserve Board's current rules on the reserves which a member of the system needed to set aside on its deposits had remained substantially unchanged for the preceding four years, except for two temporary supplements to reserve holdings on large-size managed liabilities. For net demand deposits, a graduated scale of reserve ratios, varying directly with a bank's demand liabilities, had applied to each tranche of deposits. The ratios ranged from 7 percent for minimal deposits to 16.25 for those over $400 million. Savings accounts required a reserve of 3 percent. Time deposits (including certificates) bore reserve ratios that varied from 1 to 6 percent, according to both amount and maturity. Negotiable order of withdrawal (NOW) accounts were treated as savings accounts. The law specified that reserves required on a bank's total time and savings deposits must average at least 3 percent. See Table 2.2.

The MCA not only gave the Federal Reserve Board new ranges within which, over time, the Board could adjust reserve ratios, but it specified the exact ratios that should apply to named categories of deposits after the phase-in period. Transaction accounts at a bank or thrift institution were to bear a 3 percent reserve for the first $25.0 million[11] and 12 percent for deposits over that amount. Net liabilities, if any, owed to foreign banking offices were assigned a 3 percent reserve. The Board was empowered to require reserves on a depository's *nonpersonal* time and savings deposits[12]— at 3 percent for maturities less than 18 months and 0 percent for other maturities. Except under the "extraordinary circumstances" powers, however, the Board is not authorized to place reserve requirements on personal time or savings deposits. Finally, no depository is required to hold any reserves on a certain minimum volume of reservable deposits; currently this exempt amount is $2.5 million.[13]

The term "phase-in" as used in Federal Reserve publications regarding the MCA refers to the gradual implementation of the reserve requirements under the Act, starting in November 1980. Briefly put, staged application of the new reserve ratios involved reductions of the requirements previously

TABLE 2.2
Required reserves on deposits, before and after Monetary Control Act of 1980
(as percent of deposits)

Requirements on member banks before MCA		Requirements on depository institutions after phase-in of MCA[3/]	
		All reservable liabilities:	
		First $2.5 million[2/]	0 %
Net demand deposits:[1/]		Net transaction deposits:[1/]	
$0 - 2 million	7 %	$0 - 36.7 million[2/]	3
$2 - 10 million	9-1/2	Over $36.7 million	12
$10 - 100 million	11-3/4		
$100 - 400 million	12-3/4		
Over $400 million	16-1/4		
Time and savings deposits:		Time and savings deposits:	
Savings	3	Personal	0
Time, $0 - 5 million		Nonpersonal	
30-179 days	3	Less than 1-1/2 years	3
180 days to 4 years	2-1/2	1-1/2 years or more	0
4 years or more	1		
Time, over $5 million		Net liabilities to foreign	
30-179 days	6	banking offices	3
180 days to 4 years	2-1/2		
4 years or more	1		

Sources: Board of Governors, The Federal Reserve System: Purposes & Functions, pp. 66-67; and FRB Bulletin, p. A7.

Notes: 1. The net deposits are derived by deducting from total transaction deposits (or, earlier, demand deposits) the cash items in process of collection and demand deposits due from domestic depository institutions. 2. This dollar amount is subject to minor annual adjustment. 3. Figures given in this panel of table are as of December 31, 1986.

incumbent on member banks and increases in those previously borne by other depository institutions. In determining the pace of these changes, the authorities took account of several main considerations. For the individual depository whose obligation was to rise, a need was perceived for time to adjust its financial dispositions, as well as to learn new forms and procedures. Politically, it was expedient to allow time also for state regulatory bodies to sort out their changed relationships. A quite different factor was the objective of accommodating the U.S. Treasury by not making rapid shifts in the total reserve balances of depository institutions at the Reserve Banks, shifts that might affect abruptly the Fed's net earnings payable to the Treasury.

For the existing member banks, the phase-in schedule was completed in February 1984, and the same is true of all foreign-related banks and Edge Act corporations. For non-member commercial banks, savings banks, savings and loan associations, and credit unions, the schedule of implementation will terminate September 2, 1987.[14]

Measuring Changes in Required Reserves

Having noted the narrower categories of bank deposits addressed by the reserve requirements, as well as the lower percentage ratios set, one can infer roughly from Table 2.2 that some changes in the comparative volume of required reserves are to be expected. That reserve levels relative to deposit liabilities would be generally lowered appears evident. It seems important to examine the approximate magnitude of the *effective* reserves which have resulted from adoption of the new requirements, as compared with the corresponding effective magnitudes that prevailed previously. To the extent this can be measured, it should contribute somewhat greater precision to analyzing the resulting effects on the reserve instrument as a nexus between the depository institutions and the monetary authorities. Data on effective reserves have been largely absent in studies of this subject.

Given the profuse wealth of statistical information traditionally harvested and published concerning the Federal Reserve System and the U.S. financial sector generally, one could have expected fewer methodological difficulties than are in fact confronted in this exercise. Some of the pertinent data that were regularly available monthly for many years are no longer published. In other cases, the series have been altered substantially in item definition, institutional coverage, periodicity, etc. Breaks in data series in the field of reserves and deposits were especially sharp coincident with (but not necessarily mandated by) the extension, under the MCA, of Federal Reserve requirements to the other depository institutions.

To elucidate what changes have effectively occurred in the field of required reserves over the last 15 years, Table 2.3 presents aggregate figures on Federal Reserve member banks' total deposits; deposits subject to reserve requirements; and required reserves. The effective ratios of required reserves to reservable deposits and total deposits are also given, as well as their inverse: deposits as a multiple of each reserve dollar. It has been possible to locate figures on these aggregates and compute ratios, even for a few dates after the published reserve data began merging the member banks with the other depositories, although there are blanks in some lines.[15]

TABLE 2.3
Effective levels of required reserves of member banks relative to deposits, 1969-1985 (billions of dollars; not seasonally adjusted)

	Deposits		Reserves required by Fed 3/	Non-borrowed (owned) reserves	Out-standing borrowings from FRBs	Multiple, deposits to req'd reserves		Required reserves as % of deposits	
	Total Deposits 1/	Deposits subject to reserves 2/				Total deposits	Reservable deposits	Total deposits	Reservable deposits
12/69	350.8	288.6	27.8	26.9	1.119	12.6	10.4	7.92%	9.63%
12/74	575.6	491.8	36.6	36.1	.727	15.7	13.4	6.36	7.44
12/78	716.3	624.0	41.4	40.8	.868	17.3	15.1	5.78	6.64
6/79	693.1	613.9	39.9	38.7	1.418	17.4	15.4	5.76	6.50
12/79	781.9	652.7	43.6	42.5	1.473	17.9	15.0	5.58	6.68
6/80	785.7	656.9	43.3	43.1	.380	18.1	15.2	5.51	6.59
10/80	n.a.	684.2	41.5	40.4	1.310	--	16.5	--	6.07
6/80	843.0	710.3	40.1	39.0	n.a.	21.0	17.7	4.76	5.65
6/81	861.7	n.a.	n.a.	n.a.	n.a.	n.a.	n.a.	n.a.	n.a.
12/81	897.1	n.a.	n.a.	n.a.	n.a.	n.a.	n.a.	n.a.	n.a.
6/82	915.1	n.a.	n.a.	n.a.	n.a.	n.a.	n.a.	n.a.	n.a.
12/83 4/	1,085.9	458.5e 4/	30.4e 4/	n.a.	n.a.	35.7	15.1	2.80	6.63
6/85 4/	1,179.1	n.a.	31.5	n.a.	n.a.	37.4	n.a.	2.67	n.a.

Notes on sources: 1. Total deposits from FRB Bulletin tables, last-Wednesday-series, through June 1979. Thereafter, from quarterly consolidated report of condition. 2. Deposits subject to reserve requirements from Bulletin through October 1981. See note 4 below. 3. Remaining dollar figures: from revised series on reserves and borrowings, neither adjusted seasonally nor for so-called discontinuities. 4. December 1983 figures in cols. 2 and 3 from special tabulation supplied by Board staff, slightly adjusted for size of sample. June 1985 figures also unpublished data from Board staff.

n.a. = not available
e = estimated

During the years 1974 to 1980, the actual required reserves of member banks constituted a ratio to deposits subject to reserve requirements that was quite stable in the range of 6.50 to 7.44 percent. As a percentage of total deposits at member banks, the range during this period was also very narrow, though it was in a slowly declining trend from 6.36 to 5.51 percent. Otherwise expressed, total deposits as a multiple of required reserves were slowly rising during the late 1970s–early 1980s, owing partly to the fact that types of deposit accounts carrying relatively low reserve ratios were growing at a somewhat faster pace.[16]

In November 1980 began the phasing down of member banks to the newly-lowered reserve requirements. The first step in the process resulted in reducing members' required reserves by $4.43 billion (about one-tenth) from the level that would have been required under the pre-MCA ratios. As a result, the effective reserve ratio to December 1980's total deposits dropped to 4.76 percent. Gaps in the data prevent any measurement for the ensuing three years. For the single month of December 1983, partial data made available by the Board on required reserves and reservable deposits for weekly-reporting banks, together with a published year-end statistic on total deposits, enable the aggregates and ratios to be estimated. For all member banks, the effective ratio of required reserves to *reserve-bearing* deposits for December 1983 was an estimated 6.63 percent—virtually identical with the pre-Monetary Control Act level. The other aggregates and ratios, however, show very major changes. Aggregate required reserves of member banks measured in relation to their *total* deposit liabilities had decreased from 5.50–6.00 percent in 1974–80 to 2.80 percent in December 1983. The dollar amount of deposits considered subject to reserve requirements had dropped by one-third from $684 billion in October 1980 to about $459 billion. The effective level of required reserves had fallen (in dollars) during that time span by about 27 percent, and it was destined, as the final step of the member banks' MCA implementation, for a further reduction of $2 billion in February 1984.

Put in other terms, the reservable deposits of the Federal Reserve System's member banks, which had represented a constant 83–85 percent of their total deposits throughout the 1970s, had now dropped to some 42 percent at the end of 1983. In consequence of narrowed definitions of reservable deposits, the reserves that banks were obliged to set aside at the latter date still constitute an amount legally consistent with, and eligible to "support," a volume of deposits of the *new* reservable categories concerned amounting to about 15 times that reserve level. At the same time, however, the amount of total deposits at member banks had continued to grow, and the overall deposit multiplier in December 1983 and June 1985 reached effective levels about 36–37 times the required reserve figure, as compared with multiples of 16–18 in the preceding decade.

These changes in the size of the stock of reserves of the banking system relative to the volume of bank deposits raise important questions for analysis and policy. Some of these relate to the global aggregates just mentioned, total deposits and the total reserve stock. Other questions pertain to the reasons for, and implications of, the narrowed definition of deposits now deemed to call for reserve set-asides. How does the new reserve structure compare with the liability portfolio of the banking system, or with the composition of GNP; and what might this reflect about the Board of Governors' definition of the money supply and policy targeting? We shall attempt a voyage into this territory below, after first examining the limited data available on deposits and reserves of U.S. depository institutions as a group.

Publishing of monthly data on member bank reserves and deposits was terminated at or before application of the Monetary Control Act, although some of the pertinent figures are published in year-end or semi-annual series. For the expanded group of depository institutions which that Act embraced, data appear monthly on total required reserves, but no corresponding series are published on reservable deposits or total deposits for the group. Figures obtained for this study through the courtesy of the Board staff for June and December 1984 for certain deposit categories and required reserves at a preponderant number of depositories, however, make it possible to present 1984 estimates for the total depository group similar to those examined above for member banks.

For December 1984, deposit accounts subject to reserve requirements at depository institutions amounted to $783 billion, out of total deposits of $2,673 billion. Not surprisingly, this reserve-bearing portion of almost 30 percent was much smaller than that given above for member commercial banks alone (42 percent) in the preceding year, owing to the larger share of personal time deposits at the thrift institutions. For similar reasons, the effective ratio of required reserves to reserve-bearing deposits was 5.08 percent and to total deposits was 1.49 percent (see Table 2.4). One must take note of the degree to which the new required reserve levels had been fully applied by December 1984: 100 percent for member banks and 62.5 percent for other institutions. For all depositories combined, the $39.8 billion in required reserves represented roughly 88 percent of the figure (about $45 billion) that would correspond to deposits at that date if the implementation had been completed.

It was found that the above data supplied for 1984 yielded a volume of total deposits, $2,673 billion, which is close to that estimated from different sources ($2,571), namely, from selecting and adjusting certain sub-components in the money-stock series. Employing this device, in the absence of published figures on depository institutions as such, the table gives estimated total deposits and (published) required reserves for several dates from October 1980 to 1983. It is not possible, of course, to derive a

TABLE 2.4
Effective levels of required reserves relative to deposits, all depository institutions, 1980-1985 (billions of dollars; not seasonally adjusted)

	Deposits		Reserves Required by Fed[3]	Non-borrowed (owned) reserves	Outstanding borrowings from FRBs	Multiple, deps. to req'd reserve		Req'd reserves as % of deps.	
	Total Deposits[1]	Deposits subject to Reserves				Total deps.	Reservable deps.	Total deps.	Reservable deps.
10/80	1,856.0	n.a.	41.5	40.4	1.310	44.7	n.a.	2.24	n.a.
12/80	1,966.0	n.a.	40.1	39.0	1.690	49.0	n.a.	2.04	n.a.
12/81	2,026.0	n.a.	41.6	41.3	.636	48.7	n.a.	2.02	n.a.
12/82	2,179.0	n.a.	41.4	41.2	.634	52.6	n.a.	1.90	n.a.
12/83	2,444.0	n.a.	38.3	38.1	.774	63.8	n.a.	1.57	n.a.
12/84[2]	2,673.0	782.9	39.8	37.5	3.186	67.2	19.7	1.49	5.08
6/85	2,758.0	n.a.	41.4	41.1	1.205	66.6	n.a.	1.50	n.a.

Sources: 1. Total deposits column is a summation of (a) deposit figures given in Table 1.37 of FRB Bulletin monthly for savings and loan associations, mutual savings banks, credit unions, and FSLIC-insured federal savings banks; and (b) deposits at all commercial banking institutions, given in Table 1.25 of Bulletin. 2. For 12/84, dollar figures on both total deposits and reservable deposits are as provided by FRB staff, adjusted for size of sample. 3. For other dollar series, see preceding table.

n.a. = not available

continuous series of ratios to reserve-bearing deposits by these methods. But reserve ratios to total deposits show a steady downward trend.

Analyzing the Choice of Reserve-bearing Deposits

The possible macroeconomic effects of restructuring the reserve requirements relate both to the lowered ratio of the reserve stock to *total* deposits in the banking system and to the alterations made in the *types* of deposit accounts officially designated as subject to mandatory requirements. As previously mentioned, the MCA, which had the merit of reducing the number of deposit brackets and simplifying the computation of the reserve amounts concerned, also resulted in designating only two reservable deposit categories: transaction accounts, and nonpersonal time and savings deposits. The first of these was created by adding, to the standard demand (or checking) account, two general types of "checkable" accounts[17] that had been developed and fairly well defined in the years immediately preceding the Monetary Control Act. The second type of deposit designated reservable is a hybrid, a concept rather than an account that had been previously defined and listed. Cutting across the wide spectrum of savings, term deposits, and certificates of diverse characteristics and maturities that together make up the class of time and savings deposits, the MCA coined the term "nonpersonal time deposit."[18]

It is hard to find in the professional or legislative literature a logical explanation of these deposit choices that is sufficiently clear and explicit. It is perhaps possible to piece together, from bits of scattered indications, an episodic explanation of how they were selected as reserve-bearing. At the time that the MCA was being debated and drafted, one of the major preoccupations of the Federal Reserve Board was the dwindling number of its member banks. If the institutions covered by its reserve requirements could be broadened to include most or all types of depository, the results would be three-fold: the incentive to present members to defect would disappear; the inclusion of the added depositories would produce a more uniform reserve-holding practice; and the reporting obligation on the new-comers incident to this enlargement would furnish the Board with more direct financial information. Thus, the Board was apparently more interested, within reasonable limits, in broad coverage of institutions than in broad reserve coverage of deposit types. Moreover, among deposit categories, the Fed was primarily concerned with transaction deposits. In testimony given the month preceding passage of the MCA, the Board indicated it might indeed be content to limit the imposition of reserve requirements to transaction accounts alone, given satisfactory provisions overall.[19]

The inclination of the Board to focus on transaction accounts has various origins. Throughout Fed history, demand deposits have been subject to reserve requirements, and normally at ratios much higher than those on time deposits. There is a continuing tendency to approach the subject of reserve coefficients from considerations associated with nominal maturities and past impressions about the comparative functional activity of different deposits. Apart from banking tradition, moreover, the economics profession generally regarded demand deposits as the only type of bank money used as means of payment in the process of generating GNP. Having regard to their interpretation of these criteria and measurements, the monetary and legislative authorities thus decided, albeit with some deliberation, that in principle only transaction accounts—demand deposits and the "other checkable" accounts included in the definition of M1—had a real need to be subject to the reserve instrument.

A quite different consideration arose in the legislative proceedings, however, when it became manifest that limiting the imposition of required reserves to transaction accounts (at the percentage-ratio levels under consideration) would cause an initial reduction in the volume of reserve balances held by depositories at the Reserve Banks; and that this decrease in the Fed's holdings of earning assets would, in turn, produce a perceptible fall in the annual profits that the Reserve System would transfer to the Treasury. Estimates of the prospective Treasury loss from this source ranged, under varying assumptions, from $200 million to more than $500 million per year. The Administration stated that, under the existing and prospective budgetary position then prevailing, fiscal responsibility would oblige it to oppose a drop in receipts from the Federal Reserve of more than $200 million. In light of this consideration and of the desire not to lose other objectives which were generally agreed by most constituencies for incorporation in the legislation, the Congress decided to include nonpersonal time deposits of less than 18 months in the list of liabilities subject to required reserves.

Arriving at a given level of operating profits for the Federal Reserve System could—if that were regarded as an essential objective—be accomplished in several different ways. The gross profits of the System for a certain period are determined by such variables as the amount of government securities in its portfolio, which depends on the amount and direction of open-market operations, the volume of deposits at depository institutions subject to reserve requirements, the reserve ratios applicable to those deposits, etc.; the weighted-average interest rate earned by the Fed on its securities portfolio; income earned on Reserve Bank loans at the discount window; the operating expenses incurred, etc. What is important to recognize is that altering the structure and coverage of the central bank's reserve instrument is an economic policy question to be decided on the basis of whether that would preserve the effectiveness of the Fed's monetary control policy. The matter of the level and distribution of the Reserve Systems' operating profits is not pertinent to that macroeconomic policy question. In stating that the estimated decrease in Treasury receipts was "an 'acceptable' price to pay for being able to deal with the monetary control problem," the Secretary of the Treasury was in effect conceding both the separateness of the two subjects and the superior importance of the monetary policy subject. In addition, the Secretary spoke against the notion that was incorporated in the final MCA of exempting important deposit categories from reserve requirements, noting that, in the absence of comprehensive reserve coverage of deposits, "uncontrollable shifts of funds from reservable deposits to non-reservable ones act to weaken the linkage between the reserve base and the money supply."[20]

In deciding to revise the structure of reserve requirements along the lines described, including the exemption of the bulk of time deposit accounts and certificates, the legislative and monetary authorities appear to have given inadequate attention to developments in the operational behavior of the banking industry and its depositors and to the wider implications of such changes. The Federal Reserve's policy objective of influencing monetary and credit conditions in the U.S. economy is effectuated principally through the banking system. By taking steps that affect the ability and inclination of the banks to extend or reduce the volume of funds they furnish to the credit markets, the monetary authority exerts a major, if not determining, influence on the general level of economic activity.[21] To be able to continue achieving success in this difficult task, which is subject to so many exogenous forces, monetary policy techniques must take account of institutional and operational changes in the banking sector that could condition the behavior of processes and participants in this complicated transmission chain.[22]

If the choice of which deposit types are to be reserve-bearing was made with the objective of fashioning the reserve instrument to match most closely the monetary variable under surveillance, one could conclude by inference that the chosen variable was M1. The two deposit types included in M1, demand deposits and other checkable accounts, are the only ones classed as transaction accounts; and we have seen that—had it not been for considerations outside the realm of monetary policy—reserve requirements under the MCA might have been confined to transaction deposits. In the turbulent period during which the MCA was under consideration, and for some time thereafter, the Board's focus in monetary targeting was, indeed, principally on M1. In the past few years, however, attention has been broadened to accord somewhat greater weight to the more inclusive monetary aggregates and to other economic variables.

Given the somewhat wider focus of monetary policy that has emerged, it becomes even more important to pursue the question of which types of deposit have been made subject to reserve requirements. Among the criteria that apparently were consulted is that of velocity. One customary measurement of that phenomenon has been "deposit turnover," calculated as the ratio of debits to deposits using monthly data at annual rates. Series of this variety have been collected since 1970 for demand deposits, and one on savings deposits at banks was added in 1977. Deposit turnover of demand deposits is typically at a much higher level than that of savings accounts: in 1983, for example, these were 380 and 5,[23] respectively. In both cases, the respective rate increased by about 3 times between 1977 and 1983, and the rise continued into 1986 for demand deposits. Rates of bank deposit turnover are published for only two other deposit classes— ATS-NOW accounts, publication of which began in December 1978, and money market deposit accounts (MMDA), beginning in 1983. Turnover rates for MMDA started, in their first full year of 1983, at 2.8 and have slowly risen to more than 4.0 in 1986; savings account velocity, by contrast, has declined since 1983 (along with savings deposits outstanding). The turnover rate for the ATS-NOW series has been at the 15–17 level, about 1/25 the turnover rate of demand accounts. No velocity series are available that conform to the statutory distinction between nonpersonal and personal time deposits; and turnover figures are not calculated at all on certificates of deposits.[24]

Although series on deposit turnover rates are one measure of the velocity of money, there are other indicators of greater or less relevance. Figures on the "income velocity of money" show that GNP was growing more rapidly than M1 and M2 from the mid-1970s to 1981, after which it grew less rapidly for 2–3 years before resuming at least some upward movement. The relatively short segment of the GNP ÷ M2 curve for 1981–83 reflects in part the large increase in deposit accounts of the M2 sort during the early 1980s. Since an income velocity index neither segregates one M2 component from another nor traces the behavior of personal as compared with nonpersonal accounts, it is not helpful in evaluating the Congressional choice of reserve-bearing deposits. The income velocity concept is perhaps most useful in an analytical model in which one can assume the existence of a single homogeneous monetary aggregate that revolves and interacts with real factors in the production and pricing process.

Other concepts of volatility may be more relevant than deposit turnover or income velocity rates in the context of reserve requirements—though no less difficult to quantify. The past ten years have given examples of a type of volatility, sometimes dramatic, that occurs between one deposit category and another, between different depositories, and between depository institution accounts and other financial instruments elsewhere. Certificates of deposit are issued for designated maturities, but the stock of large-denomination CDs has a maturity distribution that shifts frequently, even though typically heavily skewed toward the short term. For example, on July 31, 1985, 49 percent of the outstanding negotiable CDs owed by large commercial banks would mature within 3 months and the weighted average maturity was 5.1

months, whereas 18 months earlier over 67 percent were to fall due within 3 months and average maturity was 2.1 months. CD holders need merely to decide not to renew maturing certificates in order to effect a large-scale transfer to some other type of financial instrument—as Continental Illinois Bank & Trust Company learned—or to some consumption expenditure, with resulting consequences on required reserves as well as cash positions. Small CDs (defined as those less than $100,000 denomination, and non-marketable) have fixed maturities and are subject to penalty-deductions for early withdrawal. During periods of marked interest-rate movements, however, holders can find it advantageous to incur the penalty if a portfolio shift or some other use of the funds appears sufficiently attractive.

Table 2.5 illustrates the type of volatility represented by rapid and large-scale shifts that occur between different classes of deposits and/or certificate holdings, using figures from two different time periods. Estimates are presented of the approximate impact of the shifts concerned upon the hypothetical volume of required reserves (assuming the posted reserve ratios to have been fully phased in). As the figures show, certificate holdings and deposit categories with comparatively low rates of deposit turnover sometimes display marked fluctuations, nevertheless, in the volume held of the deposits themselves. The above considerations throw some doubt on the persuasiveness of relying on deposit-turnover figures or standard income-velocity ratios as sufficient indications of deposit stability and much less of relying on them for excluding personally-owned time accounts from the reserve requirements.

We turn now to examine other considerations than those of velocity and deposit volatility that might explain the choice of which accounts are reserve-bearing, with attention first to the distinction drawn between transaction accounts and time and savings accounts. Figures presented on the preceding page illustrated some of the fluctuations in the aggregate amount outstanding of a given deposit class and the shifts between classes. In addition to such short-run variations, there has been a marked trend in composition of the deposit liabilities of the banking system. Data for all commercial banks show that in December 1973 demand deposits (apart from interbank balances) represented 40 percent of total deposits, and by December 1983 they had shrunk to 19 percent.[25] The time deposits as a group amounted to 3.9 times the volume of demand accounts at commercial banks at the end of 1983. Although on a slightly different statistical basis than the 1983 data just given, figures for mid-1985 also indicate demand deposits as being 19 percent of total deposits at all commercial banks.

The marked drop in the relative share of demand deposits reflects, of course, the corresponding rise in the shares of other types of accounts. In current-dollar terms, while demand accounts at all commercial banks rose during the ten years 1973–83 from $275 billion to $292 billion, all other deposits taken together soared from $366 to $1,139. It is significant that

TABLE 2.5
Volatile shifts in deposit categories, with hypothetical impact on required reserves, all depository institutions (billions of dollars)

	Amount of deposits		Net change		Hypothetical change in required reserves[1]
	12/79	12/81	in $	% change	
1. Net demand deposits	270.1	244.0	-26.1	-10%	-3.13
2. Other checkable deposits	17.0	78.4	+61.4	+359%	+7.34
3. Savings deposits	420.7	342.1	-78.6	-19%	-2.37
4. Small-denom. time deposits	633.1	824.1	+191.0	+30%	+5.73
5. Large-denom. time deposits	266.0	305.9	+79.9	+35%	+2.4
6. Net change			+227.6		+9.97
Memo items					
7. Required reserves change as recorded					-1.972
8. Money market mutual funds	33.4	150.9	+118.0	+353%	0.00

	Amount of deposits		Net change		Hypothetical change in required reserves[1]
	12/82	3/83	in $	% change	
1. Net demand deposits	247.7	235.2	-12.5	-5%	-1.50
1a. Other checkable deposits	104.0	114.3	+10.3	+ㅤ10%	+1.24
2. Savings deposits	356.7	323.2	-33.5	-9%	-1.01
3. Money market deposit accounts	26.5	185.9	+159.4	+601%	+4.78
4. Small denom. time deposits	853.9	737.7	-116.2	-14%	-3.49
5. Large-denom. time deposits	336.5	299.0	-37.5	-11%	-1.13
6. Net change			-30.0		-1.11
Memo items					
7. Required reserves change as recorded					-3.753
8. Money market mutual funds	182.2	154.0	-28.2	-15%	0.00

Sources: Data on deposits from FRB Bulletin and Release H.6, not seasonally adjusted.

Note: 1. This column computed by applying, to the net deposit change, the reserve ratios (12% for transaction accounts, 3% for savings and time deposits) specified in Monetary Control Act, as if it were fully phased in. The resulting figure also gives the impact of the given deposit change upon required reserves that would occur if reserves were imposed on all time account, not merely nonpersonal deposits of less than 18 months.

in constant-dollar terms, over this 1973–83 period, demand deposits (less interbank) *decreased* about 47 percent and all other deposits increased 55 percent. Of the six major types of non-demand accounts, all are interest-earning. Two of these six, the NOW and ATS accounts, were regarded by the Monetary Control Act as being "other checkable" transaction accounts and subject to the same required reserve ratio as demand deposits: 12 percent. While the NOW and ATS categories are growing, and during the 12 months ending September 1985 increased at a faster pace than demand deposits, NOW and ATS combined nevertheless showed a smaller dollar balance at the end of 1986 than any other deposit category, except the slowly declining conventional savings accounts. The fastest-growing deposit type has been the money market deposit account. After leaping from zero to more than $300 billion in their first full year of 1983, MMDAs continued to grow, at a reduced pace, reaching $375 billion at the end of 1986—a level nearly equaling that of small-denomination time deposits. The MMDAs are thus about 2.5 times the size of the "other checkable deposits." Although an MMDA offers several types of transfer privileges which, in the Board's view, render it "competitive in some degree with transaction accounts in M1," it was "appropriately included only in broad money"—i.e., as a time deposit subject to a 3 percent reserve ratio.[26] For all time deposits, the 3 percent reserve requirement is applied only to nonpersonal accounts of less than 18 months' maturity.

Whether an MMDA is indeed sufficiently different functionally from the other new deposit types to render it appropriate for inclusion "only" in M2 is debatable. Deposit accounts can be classified in different ways, depending on the criteria and purposes. This is true of the certificate accounts as well. If one thinks of the banking industry's list of deposit liabilities as a spectrum extending from demand deposits on the extreme "left" to term deposits on the "right," the CDs would, on some standards, be placed toward the right. They have stated maturities, and the small-denomination certificates can be redeemed before maturity only with a penalty fee. Moreover, no one calculates deposit "turnover" rates on either type of certificate. On the other hand, the large-denomination CD is actively traded on the money market and, in terms of liquidity and negotiability, shares some characteristics with the checking account at the left end of the spectrum.

Under the behavioral conditions now operating in the banking system, the distinctions presently made between deposit types have a semantic basis too unreliable to justify such wide differences in reserve requirements. As already discussed, part of the classification problem is that one type of account may be competitive with a second one, while also possessing different features that resemble still other deposit types. In addition, there are extensive linkages. The clearest example is the link of the ATS to a demand deposit, whereby, when a given minimum balance in the holder's checking account is reached, a transfer is automatically made from his savings account. The same type of inter-deposit replenishment can be effected from an MMDA, through more or less similar mechanics. In both cases, the customer's choice is not whether to hold a demand account *or* an interest-bearing deposit; in many cases he holds one (or more) of each type. A bank's own account provisions frequently encourage this practice.[27] It seems likely that the phenomenon frequently described of a fairly stable amount of total demand balances outstanding (in current dollars) accompanied by a mounting rate of monthly debit turnover is explainable, in part, by these lateral transfers from paired or intermediate time accounts.

The relationship just described between demand accounts and interest-bearing deposits—whether by way of an occasional transfer to replenish the working balance in a particular checking account or by way of a more substantial portfolio shift by a firm in anticipation of higher operating and investment costs—is a familiar operation foreseen in the traditional view of money and monetary expansion. When investment requirements rise, the money supply is augmented by transfers from interest-earning assets and by the creation of demand deposits as firms increase their borrowing from the banking system. The traditional association of the demand for money with fluctuation in the commercial and industrial sector may well have been an important reason why, in setting reserve requirements, the monetary authorities customarily had placed more emphasis—and a distinctly higher reserve ratio—on demand than on time deposits.

What requires particular scrutiny is that the asymmetry between the reserve treatment of demand and time deposits has been not merely maintained but significantly increased since 1980. As shown, the deposits which have grown most rapidly, over the past 10–15 years, both in nominal and real terms, have been interest-earning accounts, most of which are classed as time deposits. Concurrently, these deposits acquired the means of ready transfer by check, telephone order, etc., to third parties as well as to the holder, that have made their liquidity comparable with the accounts classified as transaction accounts. The rate of growth in transferable time deposits together with what Blinder calls the "bouncing around of money demand"[28] among different types of account, led the Federal Reserve Board in 1979–80 to monitor developments in M2 as well as M1. In setting reserve requirements, therefore, the Board and the Congress might have been expected at least to maintain the same comparative coverage of deposits classified in M2 as in the recent past. On the contrary, the exemptions adopted in 1980 have removed previous reserve requirements from all time deposits except nonpersonal deposits of less than 18 months.

The exclusion of personal time deposits from reserve requirements is an action that seems to have resulted from various considerations. In his statement introducing the conference report on the Monetary Control Act for Senate approval, Senator Proxmire said, "I would like to emphasize that the new reserve requirement structure in the Monetary Control Act of 1980 does not apply reserve requirements to savings deposits or to consumer type time deposits. For a long time monetary experts have said that reserves on such deposits were not needed for monetary policy purposes. . . . This [Act] places commercial banks on a par with nonbank thrift institutions."[29] The specific expert opinions to which Proxmire referred were those of government-appointed commissions whose reports appeared in the 1960s and early 1970s. Although these indeed addressed many of the regulatory and structural problems later dealt with in the Deregulation portion of the 1980 legislation, they were not focused on the conduct of monetary policy.[30]

Nevertheless, the senator's remark did reflect a point of view that pervaded academic and banking circles until very recently. The main elements in that theoretical model were that money is basically different from either financial assets or credit; money does not bear interest and is a transaction medium that is accepted in the market without a discount. The central bank has the responsibility of supplying the quantity of money needed to permit the banking system to meet its credit commitments (earlier), or (as later modified) the portion of those credit needs that the Fed judges to be consistent with orderly growth and price stability. Investment is the dynamic factor in the economy that initiates increases in real growth rates and the need for credit. These fluctuations increase the demand for money and/or raise its velocity as the level of transactions rises. Thus the focus of monetary policy and its instruments needs to be on transactional money; and the supply of transactional money had for decades been defined as consisting of currency in circulation (outside the banks and the monetary authorities) plus demand deposits.[31]

Since the financial turmoil prevailing in 1979–1981 had produced changes in characteristics and volumes of depository accounts, it was recognized that some consequential adjustments would be needed in the orientation of monetary policy and the public's perception of it. Evidently it seemed sufficient for that purpose to adopt several modifications, partly statutory and partly in the public presentation of the Board's control objectives, to put more emphasis than formerly on growth paths of the money supply and less on interest-rate levels; to redefine somewhat the monetary aggregates of M1 and M2, with certain checkable deposits to be shifted to M1; and to extend both the Fed's authority over reserve requirements and the accessibility of its discounting facilities to a broad range of non-member banks and thrift institutions.

These adaptations, however, did not fully reflect either the operational changes that had occurred in the banking system or the evolution that was beginning to permeate monetary theory. Although monetary theory is still much in flux, and this paper is not the place to present a comprehensive view of it, two points are pertinent here. (1) While economists of various schools still recognize that even money in the narrow sense can be held for precautionary or speculative reasons as well as for current transactions, both the monetarists and the reformulators of Keynesian economics are increasingly content to integrate those three utilities into a single money demand curve for analytic purposes. This unification seems to result partly from the progressive blurring of the line between moneys and near-moneys on the supply side, and partly from parametral and measurement difficulties on the demand side. (2) Even if the stock of money, or group of moneys, were held only for effecting transactions, roughly two-thirds of the gross national product consists of consumption expenditures.

The exclusion of personal time deposits from the schedule of required bank reserves is inconsistent with the magnitude of consumption, the fluctuations in the volume of deposits held by individual and households, and the substantial levels and swings in the volume of credit extended to consumers by the banking system and other depositories. At the end of 1980, households reportedly owned virtually all of the small-denomination time and savings deposits outstanding at depository institutions. As for large-denomination time deposits, households held 50 percent of the entire amount outstanding, and about 63 percent of the domestic non-financial holdings.[32] About one-fifth of the total loans and leases of commercial banks at that date were listed as loans to individuals. Whether consumers at a given period will finance their purchases of durable goods or other quasi-investment items largely from their holdings of liquid assets (as in 1979–80) or from installment credit and other borrowings (as in 1985) appears to depend on such factors as the comparative interest rates on the respective sources of owned and borrowed funds, the tax code, the level of employment, and the inflationary outlook, i.e., considerations not unlike those affecting other transactions.[33]

Measurement of the extent of reserve coverage resulting from restricting reserve application to nonpersonal time deposits cannot be exact. A monthly series available for the past three years on interest-bearing time deposits of less than $100,000 does provide a breakdown by original maturity, though the maturity brackets have varied during this period, and almost never is there a break at 18 months. An estimate can be made for a single date, December 31, 1983, employing some of the data presented earlier in this paper on nonpersonal time deposits at the Federal Reserve member banks, and required reserves thereon for that date. Balances on nonpersonal time deposits (of less than 18 months) were an estimated $193 billion, with required reserves of about $5.69 billion. This constitutes an effective reserve ratio of 2.9 percent, a figure which seems plausible in relation to the statutory 3 percent. The short-term nonpersonal accounts, however, comprised only slightly more than one-fourth of the total time and savings deposits at member banks, estimated at about $723 billion. If the pre-1980 schedule of required reserves—which stipulated that the average ratio on all savings and other time deposits had to be at least 3 percent—had been in force, the requirement would have applied to the $723 billion, and the corresponding reserve obligation on time deposits would have been nearly four times the actual December 1983 figure.

If we can rely on the end-1983 estimates, the revision in reserve requirements had resulted in reducing the coverage of time deposits to almost one-quarter of the total. We do not know with any certainty how much of this reduction is attributable to excluding *personally-owned* accounts and how much to exempting *all* time deposits of more than 18 months' maturities. Figures based on a sample survey conducted monthly by the Federal Reserve show that on December 26, 1983, about 41 percent of all interest-bearing time deposits of less than $100,000 at insured commercial banks carried a maturity of more than 12 months.[34] For large-denomination time certificates of deposit, maturity figures are published only for certificates issued by large banks with domestic assets of more than $5 billion each. At these banks, about 18 percent of CDs outstanding had maturities beyond one year. Thrift institutions as well as banks issue both types of certificates. Commercial banks have about 1.5 times as many small CDs outstanding as large certificates; for the thrift organizations the proportion is much larger, about 3.5 to 1.

While it would appeal to one's sense of rectitude to have data available that correspond to the banking variables that are designated for reserve treatment, enough is now known to establish certain observations, qualitative and quantitative. In making a reduction in the overall deposits to be reserve-bearing and in setting the percentage ratios applied to them, the authorities have not sufficiently weighed the comparative economic importance of different classes of deposit accounts. Although their criteria do appear to include conventional measures of income velocity and deposit velocity (in terms of debits-to-deposits rates), there are other indicators of deposit mobility and volatility which seem to attract little attention. In a period in which the liquidity and the modalities for transfer have increased across all bank accounts, and in which four-fifths of all deposit balances are interest-earning, the reserve provisions seem to be couched in terms of a dichotomy between two compartmented categories, time deposits and transactions deposits. (Although the labels do not denote opposites semantically, they appear to be treated as such.) In a banking world in which demand deposits have, at least temporarily, tended to become limited working balances that the holders seek to minimize, the reserve ratios required against transaction accounts and against time deposits display a greater differential than the respective operational behavior of those deposit groups would seem to suggest. And *within* the time deposit field, the exemption of accounts held by individuals and households neglects the macroeconomic importance of the levels (and changes) of personal saving and consumer expenditure.

The Federal Reserve authorities show some awareness of these incongruities, acknowledging in passing that the bulk of deposits included in broader measures of the money stock do not carry reserve requirements and that the requirement structure is oriented particularly toward controlling M1. Nevertheless, there is a tendency to be preoccupied with trying to perfect the functioning of the M1 control measures. Simpson's study is useful in clarifying present and future problems in targeting M1. It does not appear to recognize that the required-reserve instrument needs restructuring if the reserve stock is to respond adequately in linking the banking components of the effective money supply with credit availability and nominal GNP.[35] One academic study that does mention explicitly the inconsistency in the configuration of reserve requirements would apparently prefer to resolve it by going still further in a monetarist direction.[36]

Effects of Differential Requirements on Incentives

In speculating about the possible effects of the present structure of reserve requirements on the incentives of the commercial banks and of depositors, it is well to recognize that there are two types of comparisons necessary. If adequate published data were available to compare the effective weighted average reserve ratio on aggregate demand deposits with that on *reserve-bearing* time and savings deposits, in the pre-MCA period, with that relationship under the new structure, it seems possible that the change might be moderate. As mentioned earlier, the previous schedule contained numerous different ratios that varied with maturities, volume, etc. The dollar figures on required reserves, as published, showed no breakdown between time and demand deposits. We did note, however, that the figures obtained for December 1983 showed that the reserve-bearing time deposits (the nonpersonal accounts of less than 18 months) carried about the same ratio as that for the *entire* time-and-savings group before the new Act, about 3 percent. For demand deposits, it seems probable that the average effective reserve ratio under the previous schedule was higher than that prevailing now. If so, the new structure has slightly narrowed the effective spread between reserve obligations on the two types of *reservable* deposits, but the nominal margin still is substantial—roughly 12 percent as compared with 3 percent.

For the *depositor,* the changed structure of reserve requirements should have no influence on his choice among different types of bank accounts. What does affect his decision is the set of terms now offered on the respective accounts, and the recent developments in both interest paid and transfer modalities available on time deposits clearly motivate him to increase the share of time relative to "transaction" deposits in his portfolio.

For the individual *bank,* the absence of any reserve obligation on personally-owned time and savings deposits must act as a strong incentive for the bank to usher its household customers into that type of account. The constant advertising drive throughout the past five years to attract customers into interest-earning certificates and deposit accounts, despite the high borrowing cost this involves for the bank, attests to the influence exerted by the lower reserve requirement for time deposits, on the one hand, and the bank's fierce desire to deter its depositors from straying to non-bank financial instruments.[37] A second development related to the different reserve treatment of transaction accounts from time accounts has been to provide the latter with explicit linkage to transactions accounts. In addition to the direct tie built into the ATS mentioned earlier, a bank may offer MMDA depositors extensive transfers into transaction accounts and to third parties.[38] During the first two years of this authority, a certain element of the traditional term-account character was retained for MMDA through minimum and average monthly balance requirements, but in 1985–1986 the minimum was cut, in steps, from $2,500 to zero. The combination of this low or zero minimum balance limit; unlimited withdrawals by the account-holder; and permissible monthly transfers to third parties (or to other accounts) that are restricted in the number but not in the dollar amount means that the banks have endowed the MMDA with the dual capabilities of serving both as an interest-earning conduit, or link, to a demand deposit and as a transactions vehicle in its own right.

For the *banking system* as a whole, the new configuration of reserve requirements may affect erratically the relationship between bank deposit liabilities and bank credit, on the one hand, and the monetary policy instruments of the Federal Reserve Board, on the other, depending on circumstances. An example illustrates how this effect may arise.

Suppose, for instance, that business firms and individuals increase their holdings of time deposits (whether certificates or MMDA balances) in commercial banks by $70 billion, because of shifts in their asset preferences or rising money incomes. Assume that one half of this $70 billion increase belongs to business firms and the other half to households. For the $35 billion held by individuals, there would be no change in the banking system's required reserves. The increased bank liabilities to the nonpersonal depositors would cause a rise of $1.05 billion in mandated reserves ($35 billion $\times$ 0.03) at the maximum, and less than that if any portion had a maturity of more than 18 months. The assumed numbers are conservatively on the high side, since the information on distribution between personal and nonpersonal holdings may not be firm. The banking system's augmented borrowing from depositors of $70 billion would permit additional credit extensions of $68.95 billion, after taking account of the $1.05 billion transfer to required reserves. If, on other assumptions, the entire $70 billion had gone into demand or NOW deposits instead of certificates or MMDA, the required reserves would have jumped by $8.40 billion instead of $1.05, no matter how the new deposits were divided between personal and business depositors, and the permissible expansion of bank credit would have been correspondingly less.

The foregoing simple example is confined to the first-round effects and does not take account of leakages; but it does serve to illustrate how greatly the consequences for both reserves and credit availability depend, under the present requirement structure, on the particular distribution of deposit holdings among nominally-different accounts and deposit holders. In this way, the new structure has widened the range within which the reserves/deposits/credit complex can respond to a given quantity change in the deposit element of the chain.

The immediately-preceding pages analyzed primarily the effects of the changes *within* the structure of reserve requirements, as they apply to different classes of depositor and types of account. It now is necessary to review the changes affecting the magnitude of total required reserves relative to the *total* deposit liabilities. This can best be done in Chapter 3, where the framework can be broad enough to examine the relevance of the reserve instrument to the other elements of monetary policy, and their combined role in influencing money income in the economy and other macroeconomic phenomena.

Notes

1. During the period 1974–1981, the proportion of total deposits at FR member banks subject to reserve requirements ranged from 84 to 88 percent. (See tables in *Federal Reserve Bulletin* for those years.) Data on member banks are no longer shown separately; and publication of the amount of deposits subject to reserve requirements was suspended in 1981.

2. The foregoing risk/maturity/volatility explanation for the comparative levels of requirements is more implicit than expressed in the literature. It may be inferred, for example, by extension of the logic for the differentiation that formerly applied to "reserve city banks." See Young, pp. 123–126.

3. It might be considered that a bank subject to the FRB reserve arrangements does enjoy, thereby, a sort of insurance protection, in that it has access to borrow at the discount window when under pressure. Yet its eligibility to borrow in that manner stems from its membership in those arrangements and bears no direct relationship to the size of its required reserve figure.

4. Board of Governors, pp. 65–71; Mayer, chap. 10; and Young, pp. 123–146, 170–176.

5. This fact has not been generally recognized. Even some otherwise excellent banking studies have treated the two systems only as differing in deposit coverage, levels of reserve ratios, etc. for the *individual* bank. E.g., Mayer et al., pp. 82–84.

6. The term depository institutions is defined in the MCA by references to other statutes, which have the effect of embracing "commercial banks, mutual savings banks, savings and loan associations, credit unions, agencies and branches of foreign banks, and Edge Act corporations" (*Federal Reserve Bulletin,* table 1.15).

7. MCA also provides that, if at least 5 of its members find that "extraordinary circumstances" prevail, the Board may depart from the limits on reserve ratios and types of liabilities for a period of 180 days. Under strict criteria, the Board may impose temporarily a supplemental reserve requirement of up to 4 percent on transaction accounts. The supplement would be handled separately and would earn interest.

8. Young, p. 38.

9. Other attributes of System membership, such as ownership of Reserve Bank stock, voting for Reserve Bank directors, and type of examination and supervisory monitoring, do not apply to non-members, of course.

10. Footnote 7 to *Federal Reserve Bulletin,* table 1.15.

11. This dollar amount is subject to small annual adjustments, and in December 1986 was set at $36.7 million.

12. "The term 'nonpersonal time deposits' means a transferable time deposit or account or a time deposit or account representing funds deposited to the credit of, or in which any beneficial interest is held by, a depositor who is not a natural person." Public Law 96-221, Section 103.

13. This dollar amount is subject to small annual adjustments.

14. The final stages for this latter group: September 1984–September 1985, 62.5 percent of the applicable reserve requirements; September 1985–September 1986, 75 percent; September 1986–September 1987, 87.5 percent; thereafter, 100 percent. Some institutions in Hawaii were granted a phase-in schedule extending to 1992.

15. (a) The Banking Section, Division of Research and Statistics of the Board of Governors, assisted by providing the figure on member banks' required reserves for December 1983. Also, it supplied a print-out of depository institutions' required reserves for the two reservable components for June and December 1984, along with parts of the corresponding data needed on deposit aggregates. Other figures were estimated, wherever possible, as indicated (Tables 2.3 and 2.4). (b) Note that the figures used for deposits are taken from the last-Wednesday-of-the-month series, whereas those for required reserves, taken from other standard FRB series, are monthly averages. For some purposes (e.g., microscopic study of detailed movements *within* a given month), one might challenge the time congruence. The series are acceptable for the present purpose, however, which is to measure changes in relative levels over much longer periods.

16. An exception to this trend occurred briefly in the period November 1978 to mid-1980, when managed liabilities rapidly surged, impelling the Board temporarily to impose supplementary and marginal reserve requirements on them.

17. The accounts thereby removed from former treatment as time deposits are the negotiable order of withdrawal (NOW) account and the automatic transfer account (ATS).

18. See note 12.

19. Speaking to the Banking committee of the Senate, the Board Chairman said: "Let me conclude, if I may, by reading . . . some principles that the Federal Reserve Board as a whole feels should underlie legislation in this area. First: Reserves should be applied to all transactions accounts. Some relatively low exemption level, or a system of graduated requirements for the smallest institutions, can be accommodated within this principle. Second: When and if reserve requirements are imposed on time deposits, they should be confined to short-term nonpersonal accounts and be at a relatively low level." The three points that followed covered uniform reserve requirements for all depositories, equal access to Fed services, full-cost pricing of those services, etc. (U.S. Congress. Senate, pp. 7–8).

20. *Ibid.,* pp. 56–57.

21. See, e.g., Mayer *et al.,* pp. 500 ff; and Kaufman, pp. 199–215. While the statement above summarizes the usual formulation, it should be added that Fed actions can affect the banks' inclination to borrow as well as lend in the markets.

22. Young, pp. 28–53.

23. The figure given here is for demand-deposit turnover at all insured banks. Turnover of demand deposits at major New York City banks has accelerated more rapidly than at all insured banks.

24. An exception to this statement is that for 1977 and 1978 the Board published savings account deposits and debits, distributed between "Business" and "Other." Business deposits constituted about 5 percent of the total.

25. The corresponding figures for member banks alone display a decline almost as great in the share of demand deposits: from 40.2 percent to 21.8.

26. Federal Reserve Board, p. 18.

27. "Citibank . . . customers will need to keep a combined average balance of $1,000 in checking and savings accounts to avoid checking charges. . . . Manufacturers Hanover gives free checking for consolidated balances over $1,500. . . ." *New York Times,* November 13, 1985, p. D6.

28. Brainard and Perry, p. 269.

29. *Congressional Record* (March 27, 1980), p. S3166.

30. Cargill, p. 56.

31. "Historically, the distinction between M1 and other, broader monetary aggregates has rested on the idea that M1 . . . is the medium through which economic transactions are made." Brainard and Perry, p. xx; and Samuelson, p. 263.

32. The figures cited are from the flow-of-funds data collected by the Board of Governors. The totals appear consistent with other deposit data published, but the reliability of the distribution by holder is not known.

33. One may conjecture that the marked surges in consumer debt accompanied by a very low personal saving rate in 1984–85 may be explainable at least to some degree by the combination of several prevailing factors influencing banks or householders: a high real rate of return being paid to consumers on their deposit balances, made possible partly by the lack of a reserve obligation for banks and thrifts on personal time accounts; a comparatively low interest rate being charged on automobile and other consumer loans, at a time when commercial short-term loan demand was moderate.

34. These maturity distributions vary, of course. For September 1985, about 44 percent of these small-denomination time deposits had a maturity of more than one year.

35. Federal Reserve Board, pp. 69 ff; and Simpson, pp. 264–265.

36. Cargill and Garcia, pp. 82–87. Both Laurent and Melton deal with the "universal" (i.e., uniform) application of Fed reserve requirements to all depositories, but neither one discusses the major restructuring and reduction produced by the MCA. Klein would exempt from reserve requirements even nonpersonal time deposits, so long as they are not targeted by the Fed.

37. The combination of these factors has even led some banks in 1984–86 to offer to issue IRA certificates at fixed rates for up to seven years and to lend the customer the money with which to purchase the certificate.

38. No restrictions on depositor eligibility or rate of interest apply, and up to 6 transfers per month are allowed, of which 3 may be draft, plus unlimited withdrawals by mail, messenger, or in person.

3

Effects on the Conduct
of Monetary Policy

*The first necessity of a Central Bank . . . is to make sure that it has an
unchallengeable control over the total volume of bank-money created by its
Member Banks. . . . The first question, therefore, is how the Central Bank can
control the amount of its Member Banks' Reserves.*
—John Maynard Keynes, *A Treatise on Money*

*What the monetary authorities strive to promote by the means at their disposal
is a sounder and more stable economy. . . . Money and credit are only a means
to an end.*
—E. A. Goldenweiser, *American Monetary Policy*

The conduct of United States monetary policy is an ongoing, dynamic
process involving the Federal Reserve System and its constituent bodies on
the one hand and the banking system and related money-market institutions
on the other. Policy objectives conceived by the Fed are carried out by
means of measures, *ad hoc* or continuing ones, that affect the banks. There
is both a reciprocal aspect in the relationship, and one of driver-and-vehicle.
In the latter sense, the banking system is an instrument panel containing
gauges and indicators that help to register the economy's approximate speed,
temperature, and remaining fuel, as well as the levers and control buttons
to accelerate or retard the pace or to modify direction.

While there are other important factors endogenous to the U.S. economic
model that affect the evolution of nominal GNP besides those involving
actions of the Federal Reserve and the banks, of course, the proper relationship
between the commercial banking system and the Federal Reserve's operating
controls is a necessary, if not sufficient, requisite for effective monetary
policy. The rational or optimum relationship can hardly be expected to
remain static, since structural as well as operating mutations occur on both
sides of this interface. The goal might be stated as that of making sure

47

that both the indicating gauges and the control buttons are progressively adapted, *pari passu* with the changes that evolve.

In working toward an appraisal of the nature of this adaptation, it may be helpful to start with a simple, skeletal description of how, and through what control instruments, monetary policy is thought to operate. Fundamentally, the described task of Federal Reserve monetary policy is to utilize the operating techniques and instruments at its disposal to maintain whatever degree of reciprocal tension appears necessary between the volume of reserves of depository institutions, on one hand, and the volume of bank deposits and credit, on the other hand, in order to achieve the monetary and economic objectives being pursued.[1] Every monetary action undertaken by the Fed has as its purpose to influence in some fashion the cost or availability of one of these magnitudes. The operational instruments designed and available for exerting the desired influence are:

• The reserves stock. At any given time, there is an existing aggregate mass or stock of cash reserves set aside, as described in the preceding chapter, in the vaults of the banks or as reserve balances at the Federal Reserve Banks. This aggregate is the collective result of individual banks' having applied the percentage reserve-ratios stipulated by the Fed to their respective deposit liabilities. By means of deals among individual banks, the distribution of the given total can be altered, but the aggregate amount of reserves of the banking system as a whole is fixed at any given moment. Changes in the total amount of reserves come about through the lending or sales activities of the Federal Reserve, as follows.

• The Reserve Bank's discount window. A bank or other listed depository institution may borrow at its regional Federal Reserve Bank, by means of an advance against its promissory note, secured by collateral. When the banking system as a whole increases (or reduces) outstanding balances owed to the Fed, that correspondingly raises (or reduces) the aggregate borrowed reserves and total reserves of the system.

• Open-market operations. The Federal Reserve holds a large portfolio of U.S. government securities (and to lesser extent, Federal agency obligations). By means of purchasing a certain volume of government securities in the market, the Fed can increase the net amount of reserves available to the banks collectively for use in making loans or investments; conversely, a sale of Treasury bills or notes from the Fed's portfolio causes a reduction in the disposable cash of the banking system and tightens its potential for credit extension.

• Change in reserve requirements. The Board is empowered, within limits, to raise or lower the percentage ratio of bank deposits that must be set aside for monetary purposes, with a tightening or easing effect, respectively, on the terms and availability of banking credit.

• Change in discount rate. The interest rate ("discount rate") charged by the Reserve Banks on loans to depository institutions can be altered by decision of the Board, in order to accommodate or discourage the current level of borrowing.

Although the Federal Reserve's operating instruments can be listed separately, they are interrelated and often are usefully employed in conjunction. Some of them require an overt decision by the Board, such as a change in the discount rate. A loan by the discount window, in contrast, is available at the initiative of the individual borrowing bank. The size of the reserve stock (given whatever set of percentage reserve-ratios is in effect) is mainly a function of the level of reserve-bearing bank deposits, and thus operates with a considerable degree of automaticity and exerts uniform effects across banks. Open-market operations are undertaken at the initiative of the Federal Reserve and at its discretion as to timing, modality, and volume, through a complicated decisional process directed and closely monitored by the Federal Open Market Committee.

While paying tribute to the versatile and comprehensive qualities of the monetary policy instruments as a collective group, economists within and outside the Federal Reserve commonly stress not only the degree of control which the Fed has over the open market instrument but its flexibility and precision. For these reasons, they point out, the Fed has to an increasing degree come to regard open-market dealing as its most effective control instrument. The infrequent and reluctant resort to a change in the discount rate and, especially, in the required reserve-ratios is noted; and the nearly exclusive use of open-market operations as the all-purpose tool is ascribed to its being the instrument of choice.[2] It should be added, however, that although the functional relationship between the level of money and credit and that of the reserve stock is sometimes not explicitly mentioned in referring to the policy mix, the role of the reserve mass as the ever-present anvil on which the hammer of open-market intervention carries out its work is recognized operationally.

The Federal Reserve System, as the central bank of the United States, is charged with the responsibility of providing the economy with a safe, flexible, and efficient banking and monetary system. This has entailed helping to shape the structure of that system and monitoring to assure its smooth functioning. The Fed regularly performs, actively or passively, as a banker for banks; and, though fostering the articulation of healthy private financial markets, it has the known capacity to serve as lender of last resort. Thus, the Federal Reserve exercises very important episcopal tasks of its own within the institutional structure. It also, however, has a major share in the still-larger sphere of general economic policy by formulating and executing the monetary policy that influences, together with other forces, the economy's macroeconomic course.

This obliges the Board and other Fed bodies to seek to assure that the rate of expansion in money and credit is adequate to the changing productive needs of the real economy, subject to the need to maintain price stability. There are problems of cyclical slumps or booms that complicate the longer-term aspects of devising monetary policies. Indeed, the task of formulating and achieving monetary policy goals is seldom free from unexpected disturbances arising from fluctuations generated within the economy or from exogenous shocks, either of which may call for modifications in the monetary stance or even new initiatives.

For analytical convenience, it has become conventional to adopt Roosa's terminology to denote the two broad types of monetary control posture. *Defensive* policy refers to action or sets of action that are mainly accommodative and are responding to seasonal, temporary, or relatively minor financial developments that can be handled within the terms of existing Board and FOMC policy. *Dynamic* monetary policy, on the other hand, embraces Fed actions that involve a significant change in course or in the Fed's objectives that are taken at the initiative and timing of the Fed itself.[3] Obviously, these distinctions are a matter of relative emphasis, and not sharply drawn. At certain times, Fed objectives can involve both some sustaining, accommodative elements and some redirectional thrust.

Manifestly, the same monetary control instruments described above can be, and are, employed by the Board and FOMC either defensively, to pursue an established policy path or sustain an existing set of market conditions, or dynamically, to launch a new initiative or combat energetically an exogenous shock. Indeed, while they may be employed with variations of volume, sequence, and modality, these are the instruments available, and they have demonstrable force.

Another reminder that is pertinent, before we proceed further, is that the Fed's control instruments are means, not ends. They can be used by the central bank for the purpose of attaining an ultimate result, or for producing some intermediate result that is regarded as being on the way toward, or as a requisite for, an ultimate result. A great deal of recent macroeconomic discussion has been devoted to considering whether the aim of monetary policy should be centered on intermediate goals that are relatively attainable and controllable by the Federal Reserve, such as a given level of interest rates or an approximate rate of monetary growth; or should be focused on a still-larger macro variable such as the nominal or real growth in GNP.[4] This discussion about the proper object for what has come to be called "targeting" is still unsettled and *sui generis* may remain so, since what merits the prime preoccupation of monetary policy changes with circumstances.

In any case, it should be underscored that the choice of one particular monetary target is not necessary to the purpose of this chapter. The main question being addressed is rather, given the present composition of the depository components in the money stock and given the present configuration of the Federal Reserve's control instruments, has the task of conducting monetary policy been significantly affected by these and other recent developments in this field? The answer may be difficult, but the question is valid and pertinent, *whatever* may be the target (or multiple targets) of monetary policy that the Fed chooses as its control objective.

In addressing the question thus posed, we shall identify successively several situations in which recent developments mights be expected, presumptively, to ease or to aggravate the task of monetary control. In the course of this examination, we can observe some points on which the brief schematic summary of Fed monetary operations given earlier in the chapter needs amplifying in the light of how Fed operating procedures have evolved in practice.

Policy Effects of Interest-bearing Transaction Deposits

The "other checkable" deposits (ATS and NOW accounts) at commercial banks and thrifts are now interest-bearing. They are classified under the 1980 banking legislation as "transaction" accounts and are included by the Federal Reserve money-stock statistics in M1, where they constituted in November 1986 about 31 percent of total M1.[5] There is some speculation that payment of interest may be extended in the next few years also to demand deposits, which accounted for about 42 percent of M1 in November 1986.

To the extent that this practice of interest payment occurs, now and in future, the deposits concerned would lose one of the main characteristics which heretofore has been thought to distinguish transaction accounts from "portfolio" deposits. Moreover, by the same token, payment of interest would also reduce the degree of homogeneity between these depository components of M1 and the other main component—currency—thus further beclouding the definition of M1.

Apart from the definitional aspect of this development, there is an analytical point to which monetary economists have given some attention and which involves the interest-rate elasticity of the demand for (narrowly-defined) money. That is, one confronts the prospect that insofar as the transaction accounts concerned become interest-bearing they may become less sensitive to interest-rate movements in the financial markets, owing to a reduction in the opportunity cost (i.e., the income foregone) to depositors in holding transaction balances as compared with holding other financial assets.[6] In order to avoid presenting the argument in an elliptical fashion, we must point out that adoption of a banking practice of paying interest on transaction deposits is expected not only to affect the interest-sensitivity of existing deposits but to augment their volume. Interest income on transaction deposits would reduce the previous differential between the rate paid on those deposits (zero is merely a special case) and those on other bank accounts, and the rate would also become closer to the return on liquid assets usually presumed to be competitive. A tentative conclusion is indicated, on this analysis, that a transaction deposit would become more attractive than before. Presumably, this would produce a shift in demand for such balances, yielding a volume both higher and more stable (because less interest-elastic). In the words of Brainard and Perry, "By itself, this would lead one to expect M1 would be higher for a given level of market rates."[7]

Before addressing the potential implications of interest-paying transaction accounts for the exercise of Federal Reserve monetary control, it is instructive to identify more fully the hypothetical framework and assumptions within which this problem has been addressed professionally thus far. Aside from individual differences, the typical analysis utilizes a model with several common features. Foremost is the usual *ceteris paribus* assumption. In its simplest form, this is a discussion limited to the quantity and elasticity effects upon transaction accounts themselves, of paying interest on those accounts, without reference to ancillary or induced effects. This basic assumption is normally combined with the postulate that this innovation is already fully in place for all transaction accounts, as the result of some future removal of the statutory prohibition on demand-deposit interest. The former zero-interest deposit then swiftly starts earning an explicit and market-determined rate. Hadjimichalakis takes pains to emphasize that market determination implies that the banks will develop a sloping supply curve for demand deposits and that the volume and the price paid can no longer be taken as demand-determined.[8] Kasriel sees a more complicated set of forces on the supply side, arguing that the Fed is able to control ultimately the quantity of narrowly-defined money in the system, while the offering price of money is influenced by costs incurred by the banks in providing the demand privilege.[9]

Even the more complex models treat transaction deposits—as presently defined and now assumed to be interest-bearing—as the only form of money that needs to enter the model, as well as the only form of money affected by the exercise of the Fed instruments. Generally omitted also are any effects that may be exerted on the deposit rates paid on other types of accounts, as a result of introducing interest-paying demand accounts; the possible unwillingness of banks to undertake a new interest cost when there remains such a large differential between the reserve ratio required on "transaction" accounts and the reserve ratios (mainly zero percent) on accounts with not-dissimilar transfer facilities, etc. These highly restrictive assumptions are necessary and understandable at this stage of the systematic attempt to incorporate interest-paying into existing monetary theory, which is still accustomed to attribute special characteristics to "transaction" deposits. But these theoretical results seem to provide, so far, mainly a broad, suggestive indication of the implications for monetary policy.

It is desirable now to take account of empirical evidence about effects that may have been produced to date by the only transaction balances currently interest-bearing—the NOW deposits. The MCA in 1980 authorized banks and thrift institutions nationwide to offer these as accounts with unlimited checking privileges. Interest paid on them was limited by a ceiling until January 1986, when it was removed. It should also be noted, however, that NOW accounts are available to households and non-profit bodies, but not to business firms.

The hypothesis about the behavioral consequences of interest-paying transaction deposits has two aspects, which may be sequential ones: the interest-induced shift from other assets toward transaction balances, and the lessened interest-elasticity thereafter. Statistical confirmation is tenuous on both points. Data on deposits at commercial banks show that the "other checkable" balances have risen during the 1980s at a rate somewhat greater than demand accounts, but more slowly than that of MMDA. At the beginning, some NOW deposits represented shifts from demand deposits (i.e., another transaction account) and others from other bank or nonbank accounts. At $114 billion in June 1985, the NOW and ATS deposits at commercial banks represented only 7 percent of total deposits and 19 percent of M1. The deregulatory actions of January 1, 1986—removal of interest ceilings and also of minimum-balance requirements—might have been expected to accelerate the growth of these deposits. Instead, NOW-ATS balances increased in the six-month period November 1985–May 1986 by 8 percent, as compared with 11 percent in the preceding six months, before the deregulation.

There are two factors that may give a partial explanation of this apparent deviation from the expected result. First, while the interest-bearing transaction accounts grew less rapidly than in the preceding period, some categories of time deposits (notably small CDs) grew not at all in 1985. Second, while the interest paid on NOW accounts fell in 1985 (and none was paid on demand accounts), the rates paid on certificates and some non-bank instruments declined even more, and some funds from those sources apparently were shifted to NOW (but some also to MMDA accounts, classified in the "time deposit" category!).[10]

To recapitulate the empirical data cited: Since the end of 1985, NOW interest rates are free to vary, and rates moved downward in late 1985 and the first half of 1986, but they improved *relative* to other competitive rates. While these factors did not raise the growth rate of NOW balances, the volume of some competing bank and non-bank accounts grew less rapidly or even leveled. Thus, during that deregulated period a net reduction occurred in the opportunity cost of holding "other checkable" (and demand) accounts.

This may partly explain why the other checkables' growth in volume outstanding, while declining in absolute rate, moderately expanded in comparison to time deposits.

Available data seem to indicate that payment of explicit interest on NOW deposit accounts has not yet produced a marked rise in the volume of those accounts outstanding, much less any marked increase in transaction deposits as a whole. It seems evident that the relatively minor rise to date is explained in part by the facts that business firms are not eligible to hold NOW accounts, and demand deposits are not eligible to receive interest. Under present circumstances, the propensity of both corporate and household depositors to minimize the size of their demand balances—which was strongly reinforced by the inflationary period of the late 1970s–early 1980s and by innovations in the financial and communications fields—is still manifest. If the above-mentioned eligibility criteria were to be removed, as hypothesized in the monetary literature cited, it seems likely that a somewhat more perceptible shift in asset preferences would occur at depository institutions, with some shift toward holding NOW and demand deposits.

One should be equally cautious about the second half of the scenario— i.e., about the extent of reduction to be expected in the sensitivity of transaction deposits, should they become interest-bearing for all holders, to interest-rate movements elsewhere. The rate movements in question presumably would include both changes in rates on short-term Treasury bills, commercial paper, etc., resulting from fluctuations in credit conditions, on one hand, and policy-oriented changes in the federal funds rate instigated by the Fed, on the other hand. If the interest return on money market instruments is moving upward, we should expect on both theoretical grounds and recent historical experience that this would put competitive pressure on all deposit classes, not just on transaction deposits, with some resulting disintermediation and/or rate increases across all the (now deregulated) deposit types. Since some portion of holders' checking balances would continue to be needed for working purposes, the transaction deposit adjustment might involve a smaller percentage decline in volume than for time deposits. The interest-sensitivity of the demand deposits might indeed initially become lower than it was before interest payment began, as theory predicts, especially if the holders' frame of reference were confined to comparing their *former,* zero return with the deregulated rate. Market psychology often adapts rapidly, however, and demand depositors—like the time deposit holders—probably would soon regard the pertinent comparison as being between their *present,* deregulated deposit return and the rates presently available elsewhere. To the extent that the deregulated, sloping *supply* curve for demand deposits moves upward in response to market conditions, the resulting "price" determined for demand deposits will rise and will act to moderate the withdrawal of demand balances. Thus, we should expect somewhat greater stability in the *volume* of demand balances to prevail, not only because of a reduced interest-sensitivity in the demand for such deposits but also because of the increased interest-sensitivity in the supply of demand deposits.

It appears to follow that the impact created by open-market operations would be correspondingly affected. For the Federal Reserve to produce a given amount of monetary stimulus, for example, the FOMC trading desk would have to purchase a greater amount of Treasury securities than before in order to lower the federal funds rate to a level sufficient to induce the desired expansion of deposits and credit. Moreover, when and if the banking world should become one in which banking practice is to pay market-determined interest rates on all types of accounts, one could expect that the impact of Fed open-market intervention would tend to be felt among *all* types of bank deposit liabilities even more uniformly than it is felt today. If that is correct, the logic and efficacy of a monetary policy focused narrowly on M1, or its deposit components, would become still more questionable than it now is.

A further effect of interest-bearing demand balances on the instruments of monetary policy could arise in the field of required reserves. If the introduction of interest-paying demand accounts were to attract some deposits away from other types of account at depository institutions, the effects on required reserves would depend on whether the shift were within the transaction group (e.g., a move from other checkable accounts to demand accounts) or were a shift from time deposits. In the former case, the level of required reserves would not be changed. If, on the other hand, the adaptation resulted in a shift from MMDA or CDs into transaction accounts, the required reserves on the amount of deposits transferred would rise by either 12 percentage points or 9 points, depending on whether the deposit source reduced was personal time deposits or was nonpersonal time accounts of less than eighteen months' maturity.

Exempting Most Time Deposits from Requirements

The banking situation that we now examine is one that primarily results not from changes in comparative interest rates paid on different deposit classes, as in the preceding case, but from legislated restructuring of the reserve requirements that are applied against deposit holdings at banking institutions. The nature and purpose underlying the original establishment of a system of mandatory set-asides were described in Chapter 2. Essentially, the objective is to provide the banking system and the Fed monetary authorities who exercise control over the system with an economic counter-weight that responds fairly predictably to the rise or fall in the aggregate volume of money and credit. The ability of the Federal Reserve Board and the Open Market Committee to carry on an effective surveillance of the system and apply any needed stimulus or restraint is dependent in part on the known operational behavior of the aggregate reserve stock in the overall context. The Monetary Control Act of 1980 changed the configuration of the banking system's required reserves in two ways: through a lowering in the ratio of total required reserves to total bank deposits, and through a marked change in the treatment of time deposits that exempts certain maturities and certain holders. The present section deals with the control effects peculiar to the changed treatment of time deposits, and the next section will address the overall deposits-reserves problem.

In making sweeping changes in the reserve requirements applicable to time and savings deposits, the Congress in 1980 was deviating from a long tradition in United States banking legislation. The Federal Reserve Act in 1913 not only set up the first truly centralized banking system in the nation's history but established the concept of required reserves, described in Chapter 2, that forms an integral part of the control mechanism linking the commercial banking system to the central bank. From the outset, savings and time deposit accounts were subject to reserve requirements—at percentage ratios that were variable at Board discretion, just as with demand deposits, though at distinctly lower ratios than the latter. (Under the National Banking Act, which had governed nationally-chartered banks for the fifty years that preceded the Federal Reserve, the banks had been obliged to hold a different form of reserves, similar to that permitted by state governments, and with no specified distinction in reserve-ratio between time and other classes of accounts.)

With all types of deposit liability thus being covered in principle by reserve requirements, the dollar amount of member-bank deposits effectively bearing required reserves constituted a very high proportion of total deposits outstanding at a given time. Table 2.3 in the preceding chapter showed that in the 1960s and 1970s, reserve-bearing deposits amounted to about 85 percent of all deposits. The difference between that figure and 100 percent is explained by the definitions in the implementing regulation, notably the adjustment to arrive at *net* demand deposits.[11] In consequence, whenever the volume of deposits and credit in the banking system rose, a corresponding fraction was absorbed into the segregated reserve stock, and whenever deposits fell the corresponding fraction was released from the reserve stock and put at the disposition of the banking system. The size of the fraction which "corresponded" differed as between demand and time accounts, but neither type was exempt: each type played its assigned share in affecting the amount of the reserves and in giving a signal of movements in its segment of the money stock.

The decision in 1980 to exempt from reserve requirements all personal time deposits and all nonpersonal time accounts of more than 18 months' maturity appears to have resulted from a tacit and perhaps unplanned alliance among quite different ideological groups. These included banking industry spokesmen who wanted simply to lighten the reserve load on a highly competitive deposit category; a somewhat populist sentiment in some Congressional circles that exempting personal time and savings deposits from reserves would benefit consumers; and the view among academic economists—which was still widely-held in the period just preceding enactment of the MCA—that only narrowly-defined money need be the target of monetary control instruments, owing to the close functional relation believed to exist between M1 and GNP. Even the Chairman of the Board of Governors explicitly acquiesced in this exemption, as mentioned in Chapter 2.[12]

It was a not-fully-understood act of fate that this decision took effect at a time when financial developments were already beginning to render it progressively inappropriate. Interest rates that banks could pay on savings and time deposits were being raised in a series of *ad hoc* steps, and banks were about to be given a schedule for complete elimination of deposit-rate ceilings. As described in preceding chapters, the same process of change in banking practice was also endowing time deposit accounts with additional and more rapid methods of transfer. While a small portion of these accounts was formally reclassified to bear the "transaction" label, those still designated as time and savings accounts were also being accorded extensive transfer properties. The spread of cash management techniques began to add *administered* methods of lateral transfer among assets to the possibilities already available on depositor initiative. In addition, professional opinion among economists was entering upon a process, which was to gain momentum through the early 1980s, of re-examining the suitability of the various potential targets for the central bank's monetary control strategy. Among the results which were about to emerge from the interaction of the above developments would be the conclusion that the angle of vision for monetary control must be wider than M1.

How does the major restructuring of reserve requirements on time deposits affect the problem of monetary control? It does so by substantially reducing the predictability of the relationship between incremental changes in time deposits and required reserve holdings. This effect results from dividing the large time-deposit category into several groups and according these groups differential reserve treatment. In mid-1985, two-thirds of total deposits (at all depository institutions) were not subject to reserve requirements, since they were either savings and time deposits owned by individuals or time deposits of a nonpersonal character with maturities of over 18 months. The volume of time deposits thereby exempted from required reserves, $1,922 billion, amounted to 3.9 times the volume of reserve-bearing time accounts. Consequently, the effect of a given rise in time deposits on the total required reserves now depends on the nominal maturity of the accounts or certificates concerned and on whether owned by households or "nonpersonal" organizations. Given the fact that net transaction accounts presently constitute only 15 percent of aggregate deposits, this kind of uncertainty thus applies to the great bulk of deposit funds at commercial banks and thrifts. Stated otherwise, 85 percent of total deposits at the institutions that are now formally embraced by the reserve requirements and discount-window privileges of the Federal Reserve either are entirely exempt from reserves or bear a maximum of 3 percent reserve obligation. Table 3.1 shows that if all time and savings accounts, without distinction as to holder or maturity, had been assessed with the same 3 percent reserve ratio, the increase in deposits from June 1984 to June 1985 would have produced a consequential rise in required reserves of double the amount of the rise calculated on the basis of the current requirement structure.

In sum, the present structure of reserve requirements (a) differentiates, within the time deposit field, between the accounts of householders and business firms in a manner implying an absolute, categorical difference in their operational behavior in the economy that has not been demonstrated; (b) makes much less precise or predictable than previously the relationship between time deposit volume and the volume of required reserves; (c) employs a percentage ratio for application to time deposits that differs substantially from that on so-called transaction deposits and does not sufficiently reflect current professional thought about the heightened transactional similarity, if not interchangeability, among deposit categories; and (d) carries the necessity—given the recently weakened linkage between this large class of bank deposits and the Fed's reserve instrument—for an increased burden to be borne by the other monetary policy instruments.

The data in the above table, including the hypothetical calculations of alternative reserve requirements, are not presented for the purpose of passing judgment on Fed monetary control performance in that particular period, of course, but to add illustrative concreteness to the general point. If the exemptions or differential treatment of different holders of time deposits reduces the automatic and uniform action of the reserve instrument, does this mean that the Fed will simply ignore the behavior of this large segment of the money stock? Probably not. The fact that M1 in the 1980s has displayed a decreased reliability as an intermediate target for GNP has led economists to reconsider other potential single or additional indicators, including M2. We are told that the FOMC staff presents, for the Committee's deliberations, projections for about 40 economic and financial variables, including all the M-measures. The subsequent behavior of these variables is followed in comparison with their projected paths.[13] This is not sufficient in itself, even though M2 might be a somewhat better choice than M1 *if*

TABLE 3.1
Changes in deposit accounts at all depository institutions, June 1984
to June 1985, with hypothetical increases in required reserves on
different bases (billions of dollars)

	Deposits outstanding			Hypothetical change in required reserves[1/]	
Type of account	June 30, 1984	June 30, 1985	Change, 6-84 to 6-85	Basis A	Basis B
Net transaction accounts	396.6	428.9	32.3	3.9	3.9
Other reservable accounts[2/]	458.9	499.1	40.2	1.2	1.2
Non-reservable deposits[3/]	1,754.50e	1,922.0e	167.5	0.0	5.0
Total	2,610.0e	2,850.0e	240.0	5.1	10.1

Sources: Calculated from deposit figures supplied by F.R. Board.

Notes: 1. Column A shows estimated change on basis of requirements
under present structure. Column B shows estimated change if
all time deposits were subject to same 3% reserve requirement. N.B.: No account could be taken of the cut-off level
below which total deposits do not have to be reported by the
individual bank. 2. Non-personal time deposits of less than
18 months, plus net Euro-currency liabilities. 3. Personal
time deposits plus non-personal time deposits over 18 months.

e = estimated

reliance were to be placed on a single monetary aggregate.[14] It is not asserted
here that the radical restructuring of reserve requirements on time deposits
destroys the possibility of monetary control, but rather that it imposes a
heavier burden on the monetary authorities in terms of greater vigilance
and greater reliance on the skillful use of the *other* monetary instruments.

In subsequent pages, we shall take a closer look at the nature of the
monetary control procedures, as they have evolved to date, in relation to
the banking developments addressed in this book.

Required Reserves Within the Macroeconomic Framework

Data presented in Chapter 2 measured the *effective* level of the officially required reserves of the U.S. banking system; that is, the dollar amounts of aggregate required reserves that actually resulted from application of the Fed's requirements, in relation to aggregate deposits in various recent years. This ratio, which had remained in a narrow range of 5.5 to somewhat over 6 percent for Federal Reserve member banks in the 1970s, dropped as a result of the 1980 revision of reserve requirements to 2.80 percent in December 1983 and 2.67 percent in mid-1985. Stated inversely, the deposit multiplier measuring the number of dollars of bank deposits which the banking system could "support" by one dollar of mandated reserves had increased from $16–18 to about $36–37.[15] The greater part of this decrease in the relative size of the reserve stock resulted from the restructuring of the requirements pertaining to time and savings deposits, including major exemptions, as discussed above. It must be recalled, however, that some alterations were made also to the structure applying to transaction deposits. These changes did not differentiate between account holders, but altered both the number of deposit-brackets and the reserve ratios applying to them. Although data are lacking to calculate the exact change, there are indications that the net incidence of reserve requirements was somewhat reduced on transaction deposits also.[16]

The size of the aggregate stock of required reserves has diminished not only relative to total deposits at depository institutions but relative to other global economic aggregates. Table 3.2 gives the ratio of total required reserves to GNP and also to M2 for selected dates over the past 20 years, using fourth-quarter averages. In each case, the respective series displays a steady decline in the comparative size of the reserve stock. Statistical weaknesses are inherent in the ratios computed from the series on M2, owing to the changing definitions of M2 composition during this period and especially owing to the emergence of entirely new depository instruments, now incorporated as components of the money stock, that had not existed previously. If we eliminate, for possible non-comparability, the ratios prior to 1979, the relation of the bank reserves to M2 from the fourth quarter of 1979 to the present fell from 2.86 percent to 1.79.

The relationship between the total stock of required reserves and total GNP is relevant to the subject of monetary control, whether one regards the proper central bank policy regime to be that of influencing nominal GNP through the controlling of an intermediate target (such as the borrowed reserves or non-borrowed reserves of the banking system) or a policy seeking to influence nominal GNP directly. For computing a ratio series, the national accounts data, while they are highly aggregative numbers that are not free of ambiguities, do not have the same problem of changing classification

TABLE 3.2
Diminution of required reserves relative to M2 and GNP (billions of current dollars)

	Gross National Product[1]	M2[2]	Total Required Reserves[2]	Ratio of Required Reserves (%) to	
				GNP	M2
Q4, '65	732.0	--	21.8	2.98%	--
Q4, '68	917.4	--	26.5	2.89	--
Q4, '69	983.5	--	27.5	2.80	--
Q4, '70	1,030.9	618.9	28.6	2.77	4.62%
Q4, '75	1,678.2	1,012.3	34.5	2.06	3.41
Q4, '79	2,591.5	1,493.9	42.8	1.65	2.86
Q4, '80	2,848.6	1,628.0	40.8	1.43	2.51
Q4, '82	3,212.5	1,945.6	40.8	1.27	2.10
Q4, '83	3,535.0	2,182.1	37.9	1.07	1.74
Q4, '84	3,852.5	2,345.9	38.8	1.01	1.65
Q4, '85	4,059.3	2,552.2	45.8	1.13	1.79

Sources: Previous tables; and Council of Economic Advisers.

Notes: 1. Seasonally adjusted quarterly figures, at annual rate.
2. Simple average of October-December monthly figures, not seasonally adjusted.

and coverage as the M2 series. Comparable data can be obtained, and ratios calculated, over a longer period than for M2. The volume of required reserves compared to GNP (in current prices) was fairly stable in the range of 2.5 to 3.0 percent, with minor fluctuations, from 1965 to the mid-1970s. From then on, the ratio declined steadily through 1984 to 1.01 percent, and showed only a slight rise in the fourth quarter of 1985 to 1.13 percent.

The behavior of this reserves-to-GNP ratio can be understood in terms of three influences that were at work during this period. First, the income-velocity of money was exhibiting a rising secular trend, because of well-known factors such as the increasing use of credit cards and electronic transfer techniques. This trend lowered not only the money balances needed per unit of national product but also the required reserves that are a function of those balances. Second, the slowly rising share of time and savings balances in total deposits during the 1970s was gradually lowering the average reserve-ratio per average deposit-dollar. Third, the exemptions and reduction in reserve ratios embodied in the 1980 law served to decrease still further the size of the reserve stock relative to GNP as well as to total bank deposits. It seems that this third factor—the effects of which may have more than an immediate impact—offers a large part of the explanation of why the GNP-to-reserves ratio (the reciprocal of the one we have been discussing) did not parallel the path of the income-velocity (GNP-to-money) curve when the latter turned downward in 1981.

Given the substantial decline in the stock of required reserves of the banking system relative to the annual flow of national economic product—the orderly and stable growth of which is a central object of macroeconomic policy—what can be inferred about its significance? Basically, one must conclude either that a reserve stock of a larger size is not needed now (or never was?); or that, in view of the shrinkage in the reserve instrument, the other Fed control instruments have consequentially acquired a greater burden to bear than formerly.

Faced with this choice, the author is of the opinion that there is a continued need for the required-reserve instrument as an important contributor to the conduct of monetary control in the U.S.; that its functions are performed in coordination with the other monetary measures employed by the Fed; and that, to be compatible with them, it must be approximately commensurate with them. It follows that it is important not merely to maintain the concept of a required reserve but to maintain also, so far as possible, the degree to which it possesses the qualities that make it valuable. These include the attributes of the required reserve stock's being fairly predictable and controllable as to its incremental relation to money and credit; its form and location (a sterilized, non–interest-bearing fund outside the economy); its timing; and its potency (the size of the reserve stock relative to other control instruments and to macroeconomic variables).

From time to time, some economists have taken a different view of the effect or desirability of the existing system of mandated reserve requirements. Alternative proposals have ranged from schemes for 100 percent reserves against all or some deposit liabilities to plans for abolishing requirements altogether. Neither the zero percent nor the 100 percent variant has any considerable following today, largely because they could not convincingly offer the fulfillment of the criteria for a reserve system identified above. If officially-mandated reserve requirements were to be abolished, the monetary authorities could indeed presume that many individual banks would make *some* sort of provision termed "reserve." But there would be such wide diversity among banks in the amount, time-reference, form, and degree of double-counting involved that aggregates computed for the whole banking system would be as difficult for the Fed to interpret as to compile. At one period in the late 1970s, when the decline in bank membership in the Federal Reserve System appeared likely to threaten ultimately the whole operation of monetary control, the Board seemed willing to contemplate compromises in the reserve area. At present, however, officials in the Fed strongly reaffirm the importance in principle of the required reserve instrument:

> Reserve requirements are important for the conduct of monetary policy because they form the link between Federal Reserve open market operations on the one hand and the supply of money and the cost and availability of credit on the other. . . . Reserve requirement ratios dictate the maximum quantity of *reservable deposits* that the reserve base can support. (italics added)[17]

When, as in the pre-1980 years, the reservable deposits amounted to 83–85 percent of member banks' total deposit liabilities (with the difference mainly accounted for by the adjustments to arrive at *net* demand deposits), the required reserve ratios, in dictating the maximum quantity of reservable deposits that could be supported, were also virtually determining the maximum amount of total deposits that the reserve stock could support. Even with the limited number of measurable observations available for the 1980s, it is clear that the reserve base no longer has this scope and reliability. For June 1984 and June 1985, reservable deposits amounted to one-third of total deposits at *all* depository institutions. At Federal Reserve member banks, data for December 1983 showed that reservable deposits had dropped to 42 percent of total deposits, about one-half of their share ten years previous.

What this means for monetary policy in operational terms can first be illustrated by a simple hypothetical example. Suppose that in a given period the volume of time deposit balances held by households is steadily rising. These could be in the form of money market deposit accounts, short-term CDs, and savings accounts.[18] These rising personal-account balances are components of the M2 money stock; M2 is one of the aggregates being targeted (secondarily) by the Fed; but M2 as a whole may or may not be growing at the same pace, depending on the current behavior of the other M2 components. Even if the Fed observes that the group of personally-owned deposits in this example is growing beyond the target range, it will be aware that the present reserve-requirements structure will not trigger any increase in required reserves. Hence, any braking effect that it wishes to apply must come entirely from discretionary use of *other* Fed control instruments—e.g., a certain volume of open-market operations or a tightening at the discount window—that is *additional* to whatever employment of those instruments would have been needed if the change in personal time deposits had been subject to reserve requirements. It may be, moreover, that the impact of the non-reserve action taken may be less focused on the disturbing factor than desirable, as seems possible in this example.

The foregoing example of a situation which could arise in the course of conducting monetary policy is hypothetical, though it seems correct infer-

entially, given the skewed restructuring and reduced level of reserve requirements. While no explicit affirmation from Fed sources is known that
confirms a *conscious* augmentation of other control measures to take account
of the altered reserve requirements, some unconscious compensation of this
sort may have occurred. The Fed's method of reserve-targeting was modified
after the autumn of 1982, for reasons which included the perception that
the relation between M1 and nominal GNP was behaving less reliably than
in the past. This was also the period of (a) the gradual phase-in of the
revised reserve requirements, which affected the deposit-money multipliers,
especially those on components in M2, and (b) a shift of deposit distribution
toward time deposits with low (or zero) reserve ratios and high multipliers.
It appears possible that the Board's shift in emphasis since late 1982 toward
measures which "largely have reflected deliberate policy judgments rather
than an automatic response" may have stemmed partly from the factors
here under review.[19]

It is important to distinguish the situation produced by the partial or
exempted reserve coverage of deposits, at times when there is an autonomous
change in specific non-reservable deposits (as in the preceding paragraph),
from a different and still broader situation. Namely, the consequences that
the high deposit multiplier and sharply-reduced stock of required reserves
create for Fed open-market operations in general. As a result of the MCA
provisions described, when the FOMC now engages in open-market intervention, any given dollar amount of FOMC transaction carried out will have
a greater monetary effect than it would have generated previously.[20] Note
that this occurs for two reasons: (1) Because the deposit multiplier has
been approximately doubled, the amount of *additional* bank deposits permitted
to the banking system for each dollar supplied to it by FOMC operations
has been raised. (2) Because the existing required reserve stock is now
smaller relative to total deposits and GNP (than it would have been before
the MCA), a dollar of open-market operations produces a larger percentage
change in the required-reserve aggregate. Fed market operations thus deliver
a magnified per-dollar impact on both bank deposits and required reserves.[21]

This weakening of the reserve instrument (the changed relative size of
the stock and the increased deposit multiplier) could perhaps be interpreted
as being offset by the increased potency of the open-market instrument.
That some degree of compensating effect has been provided by the increased
per-dollar potency of market intervention seems clear; but whether the
opposite changes in strength between the two instruments constitute a
neutralizing offset, or something greater or less, is hard to determine. For
one thing, if the per-dollar power of market operations has been doubled
(a figure that could be inferred from the data cited on effective multipliers),
this would appear to call for a high degree of accuracy in choosing the
amount and the timing of Fed market transactions, if wide swings in the

monetary aggregates and interest rates resulting from under- or over-shooting are to be avoided. Moreover, there are reasons to believe that these two interconnected monetary control instruments can be expected to function best when their strengths are commensurate, as stated above; but the MCA acted to make them more disparate.

We shall return, in the conclusion to this chapter, to the question of a more commensurate or balanced relationship among three key monetary phenomena—required reserves, open-market operations, and the reservable liabilities or assets of the banking system—and of what form that relationship might take.

Open-Market Operations, the Major Instrument

Owing to mutations in the deposit liabilities of the banking industry, on one hand, and to legislative restructuring of mandatory reserve requirements, on the other hand, the aggregate stock of required reserves now constitutes a much-reduced ratio to total bank deposits and to the broadly-defined money supply; and a large portion of deposits is no longer defined as "reservable." We concluded in the preceding sections that these developments, in the various situations examined, alter the control burden carried by the other monetary instruments. The alteration in the monetary-control burden is not always of the same nature or direction. For instance, the exemption of major deposit categories from reserve requirements impaired predictability and produced an added need for open-market intervention to offset the removal of the reserve constraint on those components of the money supply. On the other hand, the lowering of the over-all reserves-to-total-deposits ratio substantially raised the total deposits multiplier; as indicated in the preceding section, this magnified the effect of a dollar's worth of FOMC transactions, but it thereby also put a higher premium on accurate dosage.

An alternative recapitulation would be that, in consequence of the changes referred to, the aggregate reserve stock has become both smaller in size and narrower in scope than heretofore in relation to the liabilities of the banking system and to the other monetary policy instruments, and hence the interaction among them tends to be more uncertain. (This loosening of the linkage between required reserves and whatever aggregate, or flow, is targeted for control would also act to reduce the predictability of the effects from a given policy-oriented *change* in the level of required reserve ratios.) Therefore, because of the weakened reserve instrument, the Board and FOMC may need to respond by adapting the policy mix as new circumstances require. This could take the form of changes in the size or frequency of employment of the Fed's standard techniques in the other main instruments, open market operations and discount-window terms. It may also involve other, less visible activities, such as a more detailed monitoring of growth in the sub-components of bank liabilities, especially those large ones not subject to reserve requirements.

To recognize that the Federal Reserve authorities are now obliged (so long as the current impairment of the reserve instrument endures) to rely more heavily upon their other control instruments is not meant to suggest that such shifts in emphasis represent an impossible burden. In fact, the Board and the FOMC remain in a fairly powerful position to formulate and carry out policies in fulfillment of the central bank's responsibilities for monetary control and its share in macroeconomic policy. This strength has been demonstrated by the major reduction over the past four years in the rate of price and wage advance in the U.S. economy, an accomplishment to which the predominant domestic contribution (i.e., apart from certain favorable exogenous factors) was made by the Federal Reserve's policy stance and the Board's influence on economic thought and market psychology.

Among the specific instruments for exercising Fed control responsibilities, the dominant one is that of Fed operations in the market for U.S. government securities. This fact is widely recognized. The literature ranges from a simple schematic explanation in the textbooks of the Fed's role, as central bank, in "supplying or withdrawing funds" from the banking system, to the highly-detailed description, step-by-step by telephone call, of how the FOMC's trading desk executes a typical individual market transaction. Much less is known, however, about the overall dimensions of the Fed's activity in the government securities market, in absolute terms or in relation to other economic variables, and about how this activity may have changed in recent years.

As will appear below, the conduct of open-market operations has evolved very considerably. This monetary instrument was left almost unmentioned by the Monetary Control Act of 1980;[22] but the volume and modalities of market operation had been developing over the years because of changes in the money markets through which the Fed works and because of the continuing search for improved methods of applying its policy aims. This has been true to some extent ever since the 1920s, when each of the Federal Reserve Banks separately conducted its own transactions in government securities. The more pertinent aspects of policy and execution for purposes of this paper, however, are those of the 12–15 years just preceding and following the MCA.

The Federal Reserve System's holdings of U.S. government securities (alternately referred to as U.S. Treasury securities) at the end of 1986 amounted to $211.3 billion, as reflected in the December 31 condition statement consolidating all twelve Federal Reserve Banks. This body of Treasury paper consists of marketable security issues, and the Fed acquires its holdings entirely through transactions in established market channels, not from the Treasury. They constitute by far the bulk of the System's

TABLE 3.3
Federal Reserve Banks' holdings of U.S. Treasury securities in relation to total
outstanding (marketable securities; billions of dollars)

End of Year	Memo item: Gross Public Debt of U.S. Treasury	U.S. Treasury marketable sec.			Federal Reserve Banks' Holdings		
		Total (1)	Foreign Held (2)	Domesti- cally Held (3)	$ amount (4)	as % of Col. 1 (5)	as % of Col. 3 (6)
1969	368.2	235.9	11.2	224.7	57.2	24.2%	25.5%
1971	424.1	262.0	46.9	215.1	70.2	26.8	32.6
1973	469.9	270.2	55.6	214.6	78.5	29.1	36.6
1975	576.6	363.2	66.5	296.7	89.8	24.7	30.3
1977	718.9	459.9	109.6	350.3	102.5	22.3	29.3
1979	845.1	530.7	123.8	406.9	117.5	22.1	28.9
1980	930.2	623.2	129.7	493.5	121.3	19.5	24.6
1981	1,028.7	720.3	136.6	583.7	131.0	18.2	22.4
1982	1,197.1	881.5	149.5	732.0	139.3	15.8	19.0
1983	1,410.7	1,050.9	166.3	884.6	151.9	14.5	17.2
1984	1,663.0	1,247.4	192.9	1,054.5	160.9	12.9	15.3
1985	1,945.9	1,437.7	214.6	1,223.1	181.3	12.6	14.8
1986p	2,214.8	1,619.0	257.0	1,362.0	211.3	13.1	15.5

Source: Calculated from data in U.S. Treasury, Treasury Bulletin.

Note: p = preliminary

earning assets, as well as the medium with which the FOMC engages in monetary and credit control transactions.[23] At the end of 1986, the System's stock of government securities amounted to 13 percent of the total marketable volume outstanding and approximately 15 percent of the volume domestically held. These measures of percentage shares had decreased steadily from the mid-1970s, through December 1985, when they both were about one-half of their respective levels in 1973. The small percentage rise in 1986 reflected heavy Fed buying of securities in the last quarter of the year. See Table 3.3.

The declining share of the Fed's Open Market Account in total holdings of marketable U.S. governments was matched, of course, by the corresponding increase of other holders' shares. Up through 1982, the FOMC had held the largest dollar segment of domestically-owned Treasury securities. Commencing in 1983, the amounts held by the commercial banks and by state and local governments edged above the FOMC, and several other classes of holder were also increasing. The central bank's statistical position in relation to the national government debt can be measured in two ways: by the amount of governmental debt instruments that it holds compared with the total outstanding, especially the portion of the total *stock* that is market-sensitive; and by the relative amount of the current *flow* that the central bank absorbs at one time period or another. Both measurements are important in the macroeconomic context and, over time, are interrelated. Having noted the size of Fed holdings relative to total marketable paper outstanding, it is necessary to pass on to examine the way in which the Fed utilizes governmental securities in current market operations, with reference to both volume and composition of these transactions.

As one examines the data in the next three tables on open-market operations, it is instructive to observe at once the contrasts between the moderate growth in Federal Reserve holdings of marketable securities and the very rapid growth in the Fed's market transactions. Over the 20 years from 1965 to 1985, its portfolio of government securities increased about four times in size, while the volume of transactions per year grew more than 44 times. During this period, the GNP and the M2 measure of the money stock rose somewhat more rapidly than the Fed's securities holdings.

The volume of the FOMC's gross transactions per year was growing rapidly, rising from about $139 billion in 1971 to ten times that volume ($1,363 billion) by 1981. After remaining at about the 1981 level in 1982–83, the Fed's open-market transactions increased by 39 percent in 1984 to $1,915 billion, and to $2,033 billion in 1985 (Tables 3.4 and 3.5). It is important to differentiate between two measurements of the FOMC's gross open-market operations employed in this paper. As defined in the note to Table 3.5, the term "gross transactions" refers to the total amount of reported Fed purchases, sales, redemptions, and exchanges for monetary purposes, whether through outright transactions, matched transactions, or repurchase agreements. These terms will be explained in the following paragraphs. This broad definition of gross transactions is used in the growth figures given at the beginning of this paragraph, and in Line 2 of Table 3.5. A narrower measurement of FOMC transactions, Line 3 of the latter table, is termed "*adjusted gross transactions.*" This measure is calculated in the same way as for the gross transactions, except that it includes only *one* side of the matched transactions and repurchase agreements (the side initiated by the FOMC). Measured in terms of the adjusted figures, the Fed's market operations in 1985 showed a more than 33-fold increase over 1965, as compared to the 44-fold rise of the unadjusted series.[24] Even the adjusted series rose at a rate 6 times more rapid than GNP and M2.

Before proceeding further, it is necessary to introduce the element of composition—the types of market sale or purchase—for that is closely related to the burgeoning volume of activity in recent years, and helps, moreover, toward an understanding of monetary policy operations as a whole. From the textbooks, one could well gain the impression that Fed market activity in adding to, or reducing, the volume of reserves available to the banking system is carried out mainly by occasional purchases or

TABLE 3.4
Volume and composition of Federal Reserve open-market transactions in U.S. Treasury securities, 1964-1986 (billions of dollars)

Type of Transaction, Gross	1964	1969	1975	1977	1980	1982	1983	1984	1985	1986
Outright										
Purchases	10.5	11.7	21.3	20.9	12.2	19.9	22.5	23.8	26.5	24.1
Sales + redemptions	7.5	7.5	15.6	11.9	10.7	11.4	5.9	16.6	7.7	3.5
Net	3.0	4.2	5.7	9.0	1.5	8.5	16.6	7.2	18.8	20.6
Matched										
Sales	--	22.8	151.2	425.2	674.0	543.8	578.6	809.0	866.2	928.0
Purchases	--	22.8	152.1	423.8	675.5	543.2	576.9	810.4	866.0	927.3
Net	--	0.0	0.9	-1.4	1.5	-0.6	-1.7	1.4	-0.2	-0.7
Repurchase										
Purchases	9.3	23.8	140.3	178.7	113.9	130.8	106.0	127.9	134.3	170.4
Sales	8.8	23.8	139.5	180.5	113.0	130.3	108.3	127.7	132.4	160.3
Net	0.5	0.0	0.8	-1.8	0.9	0.5	-2.3	0.2	1.9	10.1
Net change in Fed holdings	3.5	4.2	7.4	5.8	3.9	8.4	12.6	8.9	20.5	30.0
Total, transactions	36.1	112.4	620.0	1,241.0	1,599.3	1,379.4	1,398.2	1,915.4	2,033.0	2,213.6
Percent distribution	100.0%	100.0%	100.0%	100.0%	100.0%	100.0%	100.0%	100.0%	100.0%	100.0%
Outright	49.9	17.1	6.0	2.6	1.4	2.3	2.0	2.1	1.7	1.3
Matched	--	40.6	48.9	68.4	84.4	78.8	82.6	84.5	85.2	83.8
Repurchase	50.1	42.3	45.1	28.9	14.2	18.9	15.3	13.3	13.1	14.9

Source: Calculated from data in Federal Reserve Bulletin.

TABLE 3.5
Measures of velocity of Federal Reserve open-market operations in U.S. government securities, 1965-1986 (billions of dollars)

	1965	1973	1975	1979	1980	1981	1982	1983	1984	1985	1986
Securities held[1]	40.8	75.6	83.8	110.9	120.0	121.9	131.6	142.8	154.0	167.4	186.5
Transactions[2]											
Gross	45.9	268.7	620.1	1,500.2	1,599.3	1,362.9	1,379.3	1,398.2	1,915.4	2,033.0	2,213.6
Adj'd gross	30.7	148.1	328.4	769.1	810.9	694.5	705.8	713.0	977.3	1,034.7	1,126.0
Turnover rates[3]											
Gross	1.13	3.56	7.40	13.53	13.28	11.18	10.48	9.79	12.44	12.14	11.87
Adj'd gross	.75	1.96	3.92	6.94	6.76	5.70	5.36	4.99	6.35	6.18	6.04

Sources: Computed from Federal Reserve Bulletin, Tables 1.18 and 1.17.

Notes: 1. Annual figures are averages of end-of month numbers. 2. Gross transactions are totals of gross purchases and gross sales, redemptions, and exchanges for Federal Reserve open market operations, whether outright transactions; matched; or repurchase. Adjusted gross transactions include only one side of the matched and repurchase agreements (the side initiated by Fed). 3. Annual turnover rates are the gross or adjusted gross transactions, respectively, divided by government securities held.

sales of government securities on an outright basis. For earlier years, that would have been more accurate than today. In the years 1960 to 1966, for example, FOMC market operations were smaller and less frequent; and outright, one-way sales and purchases by the FOMC accounted for roughly one-half, in dollar volume, of its total activity (Table 3.4). By 1969, outright buying and selling had fallen below 18 percent. The decline continued, and from 1977 through 1986 the share of outright transactions ranged from 1.3 to less than 3.0 percent. Thus, the preponderant portion of FOMC operations takes the form of transactions in which the Fed contractually arranges with the specialized dealer at the time of the deal that the sale or purchase will be reversed within a very short, specified number of days. The overnight RP is a very common maturity. These contracts are called *matched sale-purchase transactions* (MSPs) when the initial half of the paired deal is a sale of government securities by the FOMC, and *repurchase agreements* (RPs) when the initial move is a purchase by FOMC.

Although the literature proffers very little to explain the continuous preponderance of these paired operations in total FOMC activity, explanations about how the FOMC trading desk decides whether a particular day's market intervention should be on an outright or temporary basis are more available, though not altogether uniform. The standard exposition in Fed publications has consisted in describing the outright transaction, and then mentioning RPs and MSPs as the alternative form used in the event that the need to alter the volume of reserves in the system is perceived as only temporary. Examples given of a temporary situation are periods of well-known seasonal patterns, or a time in which the financial outlook is abnormally uncertain.[25] If that criterion were applied in interpreting the statistics cited above, persistent factors affecting the system's reserve position would appear to occur very seldom. Opining on this question, one well-informed observer attributed the high proportion of temporary transactions simply to indecision on the part of the Fed's trading desk, while another tends to dismiss as irrelevant the distinction between outright and reversible transactions, on the ground that the desk could always turn, without delay, from one side of the market to the other if it wished to temporize or offset its actions. The present author, by contrast, considers that the two subjects of composition and volume of Fed market operations are dually linked, and that they should be seen as meaningful parts, in conjunction with other parts, of overall monetary policy as presently conducted.

In the group of itemized paragraphs that follows, the attempt is made to characterize some of the main conceptual and technical elements that enter into the present-day conduct of open-market operations.

• The FOMC and its trading desk perform a major share in the Fed's task of affecting the availability and cost of resources to the depository banking system. Open-market operations constitute a process whereby the

Federal Reserve carries on a nearly-ceaseless transfer of dollar funds in exchange for counters, and *vice versa,* between itself and the depository banking system. In recognizing that U.S. government debt obligations represent the most suitable counter, the Fed accepts as a tenet that the market for government paper is so wide and deep that FOMC transactions of almost any desired size can be effected without perceptibly affecting the market volume or price (interest rate).

• Yet in practice, the FOMC exhibits anxiety, if not ambivalence, about the market's capacity to absorb securities (or dollars). This may pertain especially to situations in which the Fed is acting in its "defensive," corrective capacity. Writing in 1982, Meek said that "on many occasions desk sales of $600 million to $700 million of bills would cause hardly a ripple. In more troubled times, transactions half as large could affect rates significantly."[26] For comparison with those numbers, note that for 1982 the average amount of FOMC adjusted gross transactions per working day was about $2,800 million.

• Susceptibility of the market to price effects from FOMC operations seemingly is perceived by the Fed to be greater for outright transactions. Apparently the reason is that those are accomplished by a single one-way, market-wide solicitation, whereas an MSP or RP constitutes a sale or purchase agreement paired with an assured reversal, at a pre-negotiated price and between the same parties. If there is a firm intention that there will be a virtually immediate reversal of a given exchange, the RP/MSP technique avoids the uncertainties involved in a second market solicitation—to find willing parties and set the interest/price—for the reversing transaction. The practice and predilection of FOMC in favor of these paired temporary transactions have become so established that the trading manager is inclined to make an outright deal only after seeking express permission from the Board Chairman.[27]

• Examples of reversible securities transactions that FOMC performs in the defensive[28] portion of its role are ones that enable the banks to acquire additional reserves for a day or so at the end of a maintenance period to avoid a shortfall that, according to Fed estimates, might otherwise occur in their average level of required reserves; or transactions that help government securities dealers temporarily to finance their inventories. These dealers customarily carry very small portfolios in their own names, and act as brokers. For the banks or dealers, the main alternative source for overnight borrowing would be the federal funds market, and both alternatives have attractions. Deals in the funds market are exempt (to both parties, if banks) from reserve requirements; on the other hand, an RP (if overnight) is also reserve-exempt, and the RP interest rate on FOMC transactions seems to lie some 25 to 100 basis points below the prevailing federal funds rate. From the standpoint of the parties with whom the FOMC contracts, these and other financing sources offer a range of available choices for meeting their needs.

• From all evidence, it is clear that the FOMC desk sets itself the goal of carrying on its surveillance of the money market and the economy in a manner constant and responsible. The orientation includes not only monitoring the relationship between observed numbers and the Fed's projected paths but also listening for discerned or suspected signals emanating from the markets themselves. The possibility even exists that the concern to anticipate and meet temporary situations might, to some degree, be overly zealous. To the extent that occurs—and it is difficult to measure—the Fed becomes the lender or borrower of *first* resort.

• In the course of applying any of the regimes that it has employed over the past 25 years for achieving its control objectives, the Fed has always accorded a very prominent position to the subject of reserves, in principle and practice. Recognition of the conceptual relationship between the banking system's reserves and the volume of money and credit is reflected both in the mandated reserve requirements to which banks are subject and in the operational actions undertaken by the Fed. Whether the operating regime is one in which the designated intermediate target is the federal funds rate, unborrowed reserves, or borrowed ones, it is axiomatic that all control measures taken by the Fed operate directly or indirectly by affecting the quantity and cost of reserves. It is somewhat surprising, however, that the central bank exhibits some ambivalence in this field. On one hand, those deposit liabilities that are reservable by law are closely monitored, with reserve-maintenance periods short enough to reflect deposit fluctuations; and deficiencies in meeting reserve requirements incur penalty payments. On the other hand, the authorities are aware of the banks' desires and stratagems to devise forms of holdings and transactions that avoid the incurring of reserve obligations. Some of these devices are practices between the banks and their non-bank customers, such as deposit-sweeping and other forms of cash management in which the Fed does not directly participate. Other ways in which reserve-holding is minimized include the statutory exemption of large categories of time deposits, as well as the Fed's extensive use of RPs and MSPs. While RPs and MSPs are indeed initiated by the FOMC, by reason of its own perception of how the aggregates are likely to move, they also serve accommodatively to some extent to ease the banks' reserve burdens.

• The Fed's more dynamic objectives also contribute to the high proportion of market interventions of the RP-MSP type and the increased volume and faster pace of its market operations overall. Data presented in Table 3.6 show that FOMC operations, even if measured on the adjusted gross basis, have expanded much more rapidly than M2 and GNP (and, *a fortiori,* than M1). The question of how to quantify the Federal Reserve's open-market

TABLE 3.6
Comparative growth of GNP and Federal Reserve open-market operations
(billions of current dollars)

	Gross national product	Fed market operations		Index, 1965 = 1.00	
		Gross Operations	Adj'd gross Operations	GNP	Adj'd gross Operations
1965	705.1	45.9	30.7	1.00	1.00
1968	892.7	84.5	68.5	1.27	2.23
1969	963.9	112.4	65.8	1.37	2.14
1971	1,102.7	138.8	79.1	1.56	2.58
1975	1,598.4	620.1	328.4	2.27	10.70
1979	2,508.2	1,500.2	769.1	3.56	25.05
1980	2,732.0	1,599.3	810.9	3.87	26.41
1981	3,052.6	1,362.9	694.5	4.33	22.62
1982	3,166.0	1,379.4	705.8	4.49	22.99
1983	3,405.7	1,398.2	713.0	4.83	23.22
1984	3,765.0	1,936.2	987.2	5.34	32.16
1985	3,988.1	2,033.0	1,034.7	5.66	33.70
1986	4,206.1p	2,213.6	1,126.0	5.97	36.68

Sources: Computed from previous tables; GNP data from Council of
          Economic Advisers.

Note: p = preliminary

operations is a matter of judgment and purpose. Young chose to exclude
RPs and MSPs altogether, after some hesitation, as being technical "transient
market accommodations."[29] For the years 1961–71, which he was addressing,
that may have seemed appropriate, particularly if the purpose was to indicate
the annual net change in Fed securities holdings. But given the enormous
growth in the absolute and relative amount of these reversible transactions
and the fact that, in electing to make an RP or MSP, the FOMC desk is
usually choosing between doing that and making an outright transaction,[30]

one may conclude that Fed market activity in attempting to control its intermediate and ultimate economic targets would be seriously understated if it were to be measured only by outright transactions.

• In observing the mounting volume of Federal Reserve open-market activity, the preceding paragraphs have noted the changed maturity composition of these operations. We have also seen that transactions executed by the FOMC have increased at a faster pace than either gross national product or the M1 and M2 monetary aggregates—which are generally regarded as being among the ultimate and the intermediate targets, respectively, of monetary policy. In Figure 3.1, the adjusted gross FOMC market transactions are compared, on a ratio scale, with two other banking variables of monetary interest: gross debits to demand deposits at banks, and required reserves.[31] The volume of FOMC transactions rose steeply in the years 1973 through 1977, at a rate even higher than that of demand-deposit debits. The 1970s were a period of persistent inflation and of expanding economic activity (except for the recession of late 1974–75), and the bank debits accelerated again from 1978 onward, taking the lead in growth from the FOMC series through 1983. A further factor influencing the behavior of the bank debits curve is that, beginning at the end of the 1960s, demand deposits outstanding have been smaller in volume and slower in growth than time deposits. We have commented earlier on the reasons bearing on the level and growth in demand balances. The high rates of price increase combined with slow increase in demand balances outstanding in the 1970s–1980s resulted in a stagnant or declining *real* volume of demand deposits. Depositors compensated for their surging level of debit and credit transactions by a more rapid turnover of their account balances.

As to the behavior of the FOMC's adjusted gross transactions in the 1980s, several factors seem to have been operative. These can be better understood if we consider the curves on open-market transactions and required reserves in relation to each other. The data plotted for required reserves show the annual average levels of required holdings for *member* banks for 1970–1980 inclusive, and thereafter the holdings of *all* depository institutions. It is not merely that this is the only way in which the data are published, as noted in Chapter 2, but the series as here presented constitutes, for both periods, the series of mandatory reserve balances over which the Federal Reserve Board had jurisdiction at the respective dates. As the reader will recall, moreover, implementation of the Monetary Control Act provided for a downward revision of member banks' reserve obligations over about three years ending in early 1984, and for a six-year phasing in of the requirements for thrift institutions and nonmember banks, with the combined end-result to be a lower level of required reserves relative to total deposits than pre-MCA. Many of the Fed's defensive open-market operations relate in one way or another to the various reserve aggregates, among which

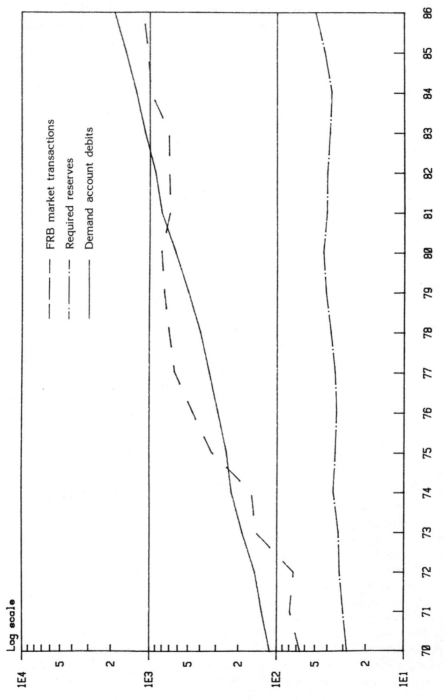

Figure 3.1 FRB market transactions compared to required reserves and demand account debits

the required-reserves figure is a key number. The flat portion of the FOMC curve for 1981 through 1983 seems explainable in large part by the transition to absolute and relative reserve reductions. (Note that the curve on required reserves resumed in 1985 an upward movement from its new, reduced level.)

Another reason for the flat shape of the open-market activity curve in the early 1980s seems to be that during that period some of the FOMC's matched and repurchase transactions were contracted for a slightly longer period than the typical one-day maturity, which is sometimes renewed. Once again, that was to some extent related to the transition in reserves. The author cannot quantify this factor, and the same is true of the effect of changes in the Treasury's handling of its balances at commercial banks, though both of these items had at least some influence, according to Fed sources.

• Many FOMC transactions represent an intervention made when the actuals of the economic variables concerned deviate from the range of projected or desired values, or seem about to deviate. Prior to 1982, corrective moves in the market tended to be taken rather automatically, in order to keep a given interest rate or monetary aggregate—e.g., the federal funds rate or the amount of unborrowed reserves—within a narrow range prescribed by the Committee. Under recent policy regimes permitting greater scope for deliberate or discretionary reaction to such departures from path, the trading desk's responses have been guided by a more judgmental interpretation of FOMC instructions.[32] This greater exercise of discretion, as compared with "rules," does not appear to reflect any increased confidence by the Fed in the market's ability for satisfactory self-correction, however.[33]

• *In sum*, the general conduct of Federal Reserve monetary policy in the mid-1980s displays a greater recognition of the decreased significance of M1, especially as to its functional relation to GNP, than it did eight-ten years ago. In partial acknowledgment of this recognition, it shows willingness to use discretion in amending projected monetary growth paths—in addition to adjusting its "instrument settings"—in response to unforeseen economic developments or exogenous shocks. In the process, the Fed is not averse to extending, if necessary, the field of vision and time-frame of its policy surveillance. These manifestations show both pragmatism in the monetary context and a sense of current macroeconomic responsibility. That is, the Fed's recent behavior is partly dictated by the prolonged absence of an appropriate governmental fiscal policy domestically and also by the Fed's concern over the serious distortions internationally in exchange rates, payments balances, growth rates, and debt burdens.

Nevertheless, despite this degree of flexibility and awareness of broad obligations, the structural design of the Federal Reserve's control system has not been fully adapted to the breadth of Fed tasks and to the altered banking world with which it deals. The focus remains principally on intermediate aggregates, and on M1 in particular.[34] Indeed, in some ways, notably in the dismantling of reserve requirements for a broad range of deposits, the monetary controls have become less well adapted in the 1980s.

The immediately preceding section endeavored to characterize the present-day conduct of open-market operations, both as to its dimensions and composition and as to the concepts and objectives from which it proceeds. As this examination shows, the Board and the FOMC are engaged in carrying on a very active, and managed system of monetary control. The objectives are the well-recognized ones of influencing the money supply and interest rates, both for the direct effects of the actions in maintaining satisfactory conditions in the financial markets and for their ultimate effects on the volume of credit and national product. Dimensions have become very large. Market intervention by the FOMC in 1986 amounted to about $4.5 billion per business day. Measured annually rather than on a per-day basis, the 1986 open-market transactions, at $1,126 billion, corresponded to over 26 percent of GNP.

Although the volume of open-market intervention by the Federal Reserve has grown more rapidly than either the M2 money stock or GNP, total activity in the U.S. government securities market has out-paced the Fed. Published data do not permit a comparison of transactions of *all* types by the FOMC with the corresponding volume in the entire market, but the FOMC share in *outright* transactions alone can be calculated. In the early 1970s, outright purchases and sales by the FOMC desk accounted for about 3 percent of such market transactions, as reported to the New York Federal Reserve Bank. By 1985 and 1986, the absolute dollar volume of the central bank's outright operations had not altered significantly, but participation from other holders of U.S. government securities had skyrocketed (see Table 3.7). This reflected the greatly increased volume of marketable government paper issued and outstanding in the hands of all holders, foreign and domestic. The FOMC's proportionate share in daily outright transactions therefore fell from 3 percent in 1974 to 0.2 percent in 1985 and 0.1 percent in 1986.[35] While the FOMC share in the market volume of RPs and MSPs may have declined less precipitously than in the outright category (since the bulk of the FOMC's mounting intervention has been of the RP-MSP type), it probably sustained some relative decrease there also.

Concluding Observations

The factual situation that emerges from this study is one in which the Federal Reserve is engaged in a high and increasingly difficult amount of activity in fulfilling its dual responsibilities in the financial system and in the conduct of U.S. macroeconomic policy. This stems from a progressive

TABLE 3.7
FOMC share in total outright transactions on U.S. government securities market (averages of daily figures; millions of dollars)

	1974	1978	1982	1983	1984	1985	1986
All outright transactions[1/]	3,580	10,285	32,271	42,135	52,778	75,331	95,422
By FOMC[2/]	95	160	124	113	160	136	110
Share of total	2.7%	1.6%	0.4%	0.3%	0.3%	0.2%	0.1%

Source: Computed from tables in Federal Reserve Bulletin.

Notes: 1. Gross purchases and sales of specialized dealers in government securities reporting to N.Y. Federal Reserve Bank. Redemptions and exchanges not included.
2. FOMC transactions do include redemptions; FOMC daily figures are published annual totals divided by 252.

rise in both defensive and dynamic monetary actions considered necessary to cope with a banking system whose deposit liabilities have changed in their functional attributes as well as in their relation to the reserve instrument; an economy in which other sources of credit less subject to Fed control have proliferated domestically and abroad; and a governmental fiscal policy stance that is almost chronically pro-cyclical. Some of these developments have been treated in depth in this paper, and others are identified to greater or lesser extent in passing.

Although the monetary control activity of the Federal Reserve—particularly as measured by its most-used instrument, open-market intervention—has grown markedly in the volume of transactions as well as in portfolio turnover, total private operations in the nation's banking and other financial markets have expanded at a pace at least as rapid, and have become more international. This is indicated by such diverse gauges as the high activity in the market for government securities, the deposit turnover rate at banks, and the birthrate of new trading markets and financial instruments. One widely-recognized result of this whole process, directly in the monetary sphere, has been to compromise the reliability of the functional chain on the basis of which monetary policy-making has for so long proceeded: reserve aggregate/transaction deposits/M1/credit/GNP. Each one of the elements in the chain has been affected in some way that either distorts the linkage to the next link or renders the original link no longer the unique connection but only one of several.

While the Depository Institutions Deregulation and Monetary Control Act of 1980 was mainly concerned with gradual elimination of interest-rate ceilings on bank deposits and broadening the asset choices for thrift institutions, it did make a limited contribution to monetary control. By bringing all commercial banks and savings institutions under the same reserve requirements as Federal Reserve System members, the Act added a somewhat greater uniformity of competitive conditions at the individual bank level. That enlargement could also have served to augment the Fed's ability to predict the global relation between money and credit, on one hand, and the stock of required reserves, on the other hand. At the same time, unfortunately, the MCA caused serious damage to predictability by completely exempting huge classes of deposit accounts from reserve requirements. Moreover, the trend in financial markets is toward non-deposit liabilities and other transactions, both customary and innovative, that are less exposed to the monetary policy instruments. This latter phenomenon, while recognized among experts, has not been dealt with by statutory or administrative action.

It is instructive for one's perspective to be reminded that a few of the altered banking practices of the past several years are not unprecedented in American financial history. Merris and Wood have assembled evidence showing that some among the many financial innovations are reversions to activities that, to some degree, existed during the decade of the 1920s. The list included payment of interest on interbank deposits and on ordinary demand deposits; rapid growth of time deposits, sometimes with transfer options; resort to variable-rate loans, call loans, and a shortening of loan maturities; and bank borrowing of federal funds. Some of those practices in the 1920s were mainly confined to the large New York City banks and, as the authors point out, the competition for non-deposit funds in the 1980s has gone "far beyond the point at which it was interrupted in 1930."[36] There is no doubt that the years ending in 1930–31 were innovative and turbulent. To be reminded of some rough similarities between the 1920s and the 1980s is helpful to the analytical process (and, for some persons, sobering).

The first two paragraphs of this concluding section restate, in briefer and different terms, the broad problem that is being addressed throughout this study: What changes have occurred, in banking practices and in the relationship of the banking system to the Federal Reserve, that may affect the conduct of monetary control policy? In the present chapter, we have identified several such changes which, if the analysis is correct, do indeed appear to place a heavier burden on the Fed's control instruments. In addition to the mutations in behavioral properties of bank deposits and the restructuring of reserve requirements, which have received primary attention in this study, other changes represent a much-intensified use of earlier practices, including such non-deposit and non-reservable sources of borrowing as repurchase agreements and federal funds. Still others constitute transactions that, although large in volume, do not even appear on the balance sheet, such as daily sweeping arrangements on demand accounts. Addressing the full scope of this "explosion in new financial market practices and instruments"[37] which the Federal Reserve's control system must somehow take into account, one is led to ask whether steps could usefully be taken in the United States to bring about a still better adaptation in the monetary control area.

It is well to recognize that the monetary problems addressed in this study are not unique to the U.S. Both in the evolution of banking and capital markets and in the changing nature of the relation between the banking system and the central banking authority, there are many elements of similarity among the principal industrial countries. All members of the Organization for Economic Cooperation and Development (OECD) have had access to the same technological advances, and the progressive liberalization of international trade and payments has both permitted a rising flow of goods and financial services and sharpened its competitiveness. The domestic forces which were already putting upward pressure on prices in the early 1970s were heavily reinforced by the exogenous shocks from the oil market. Generated during the inflationary climate which followed, a result common to all countries has been a much higher mobility of funds, stemming partly from the increased desire of both lenders and borrowers to regard (and treat) all financial instruments as marketable.[38] Innovations in electronic communication and data processing have greatly facilitated the restless search for almost hourly profit maxir..ization.

In responding to the changed situation, monetary authorities of the major nations, while mutually learning from their consultations together, have necessarily proceeded within the institutional arrangements and differing economic circumstances in their respective countries. Central banks have traditionally played an important role in policy making, particularly with reference to price stability, the balance of payments, and exchange rates. Those subjects typically have commanded a higher priority in other developed countries than in the U.S., owing to the greater exposure to which their economies were subject because of the high ratios between their foreign trade-related payments and gross domestic product. Those factors, combined with the fact that in some economies there was only a meagre volume of marketable governmental paper for secondary trading, help to explain that the planning and execution of monetary policy were centered on credit ceilings or quotas, administrative controls on interest rates, interest targeting, capital market rationing, and foreign exchange market intervention. Except for the United States and Britain, open-market operations by the central bank were very limited or non-existent. Reserve requirements were more common, but usually in the form of prescribed "portfolio" investment in designated assets, rather than of balances sequestered outside the economy.

Monetary policy practiced by foreign central banks has altered appreciably since the early or mid-1970s. Persistent inflationary pressures during most of the period not only produced the rapid financial innovation and heightened volatility mentioned above but added to the burden on monetary policy resulting from governmental deficits in many countries. Briefly summarized, the major policy adaptations have been the following. Use of monetary aggregates grew during the period, and about half of the OECD members now employ some form of monetary targeting. This is attributed to the close relation of money growth to prices (and, for some periods, to national product) as well as to the difficulty during inflationary surges of determining what interest rate to target. The similar difficulty faced in defining money, however, is already leading some authorities now to make their monetary targeting less precise. In general, quantitative credit controls and administrative controls of all sorts have been downgraded. This results from their having proved increasingly difficult to enforce and from the growing breadth and sophistication of markets. This latter factor has permitted the central bank in some nations to make a limited use of some form of intervention using domestic securities, but there are very few countries in which regular, official operations in a secondary market is a major instrument affecting liquidity of the system. By contrast, intervention on the foreign exchange market remains an active form of monetary policy for domestic stabilization as well as balance-of-payments purposes. In regard to minimum required reserves, some countries have moved from treating certain asset holdings as acceptable to requiring reserves in the form of balances at the central bank, thus partially resembling the traditional American system. In contrast to recent U.S. developments, however, in some nations the authorities, for the purpose of adapting to change and improving monetary control, have extended the scope of their reserve requirements to additional financial instruments and institutions, coupled with some lowering of the reserve ratios.

In sum, in adapting their policy planning and implementation, monetary authorities of the industrial countries appear to recognize that the mutations in financial practices of the banking system have emanated from motives of bank as well as non-bank participants and that the *form* of a particular innovation was shaped, of course, by various effforts to improve the risk/ benefit ratio—including the effort by financial institutions to reduce their exposure to monetary policy instruments.

Recommendations

As stated earlier, the objective of this study has been to examine selected changes in the banking system that appear to be of a continuing or long-term nature and that are of importance to the relationship between the financial institutions and the Federal Reserve in its monetary policy role. The approach has been descriptive and analytical of the changes and present status of the two participants in this relationship, rather than normative. This decision still appears valid for the paper itself and its possible use by others. At the same time, there are grounds at this stage for seeking to use the findings of this research to suggest, in a broad manner, areas in which the relationship could be made still more effective in the interest of macroeconomic policy.

The present time seems both opportune and desirable for a constructive review of this relationship, for several reasons. First, the Federal Reserve itself during the past 10–12 years has been re-examining its policy planning and operations, having made the experience of three somewhat different operating regimes. The Fed and its observers have the benefit of searching professional debate and research during this decade on the principles and practice involved in monetary control. Moreover, the effects of the 1980 and 1982 banking legislation and of recent financial market developments, while not fully visible, can now be discerned well enough and should be taken into account consciously, before unforeseen domestic and external market events or legislation produce further complications.

In the points presented below, the main emphasis is placed on the general statement of the problem or objective. In some cases, that is followed by a more specific suggestion for consideration. The several points are thought to be mutually compatible and some are inter-connected; but they are not necessarily a package.

1. *The Fed's ultimate economic objectives.* The problem here is two-fold: What should be the targets of macroeconomic policy in the long run; and how should the Fed conciliate its aims with the fiscal and other national authorities?

• For the ultimate or long-term goals of national economic policy, the Fed does not and can not have a single guide or objective. Within the formulation process, however, the concept of plural objectives should be more consciously and frankly embraced. A major target is now commonly agreed among economists to be the nominal rate of GNP growth. It seems inescapable, moreover, that the Fed Board be concerned with *both* the quantity and the price components of GNP in its own deliberations and in concerting with other Washington authorities. Realistic division-of-labor con-siderations—and political prudence—suggest that the Federal Reserve should not be regarded publicly as an agency *establishing* the nation's GNP target. The Fed should be free to pursue a discretionary policy, through actions influencing money and credit aggregates and interest rates, designed to facilitate achievement of reasonably sustainable (real) growth rates and stable price levels. See also Points 5 and 7 below.

• Added to the ultimate objectives for domestic prices and national product are some highly relevant *international* concerns. The Board and FOMC already look at projections of the balance of payments. Findings of the Study Group appointed by central banks of the Group of Ten confirm that the heightened global mobility of capital and the regime of fluctuating exchange rates, taken together, make the external economic sector a much more important consideration and potential constraint for national monetary policy than formerly. Without necessarily adopting a fixed rate or even a "target zone" for the dollar, the Board and the Treasury clearly need to incorporate an intelligent view about the coherence of currency relationships into the ultimate objectives.

2. *Shorter-term objectives.* Some questions often discussed under this heading concern technical operating issues that are only peripheral to the subject addressed in this study. E.g., whether the monetary variable that the Fed chooses to "target" is borrowed reserves, unborrowed reserves, or the federal funds rate is not directly relevant to considering whether the Fed's monetary control instruments could be better adapted for use in *any* of those operating regimes. The changes suggested below have a bearing on improving the Fed-banking system relationship, for the short-term as well as ultimate orientation of policy.

Several of these modifications are aimed at strengthening a particular monetary policy instrument or at achieving a better balance among the ensemble:

3. *Closing the gaps in deposit coverage.* The criterion of *controllability* is often cited in discussions about what variables should be targeted and the techniques for the Fed to employ. The fact that some economic variables are not fully subject to the Federal Reserve's control does not diminish, but heightens, the need to optimize the Fed's relation to those deposit liabilities that are well within its recognized reach. This study has demonstrated that as an outcome of the 1980 legislation all time and savings deposits except for nonpersonal accounts of less than 18 months are exempt from Federal Reserve Board reserve requirements, with the result that four-fifths of all time deposits and two-thirds of total deposit balances at depository institutions are not reflected in the reserve stock that is so central to the operation of the U.S. monetary control system. Of the various conceivable ways of remedying this defect, the following is recommended for consideration here.

• The simplest, most modest correction would be to make all time (including savings) accounts subject to a uniform 3 percent reserve coefficient to deposits, without regard to type of owner or maturity. This would in effect recognize that the "moneyness" of household time balances may not differ much from nonpersonal balances; and that, with the very liberal transfer features now prevailing, the stated maturity of a deposit or certificate is hardly binding. Note that this solution would tacitly accept (as the existing structure does) the past wisdom that time deposits have only a portfolio character and hence should be subject to a reserve coefficient much lower than that on demand deposits. See also Point 5.

4. *The reserve stock and open-market intervention.* By eliminating the exemptions in the present requirement structure as proposed above, the authorities would assure that a net rise or fall in any category of deposit would engender a consequent, known change in required reserves against

those deposits. Restoring this parallelism of response would improve the predictability of the monetary aggregates' behavior. A related but separate result would be that (assuming no other alterations in the requirements structure) the total reserve stock would rise. One might surmise that the new level of reserves relative to total deposits for FRS member banks would be about the same or slightly below the pre-1980 level, and for thrift institutions somewhat above that level. In view of the high volume of open-market intervention in recent years and the much-augmented rate of financial market activity, some of which is neither subject to reserve requirements nor reflected in accounting statements, attainment of a total reserve stock more commensurate in weight with the open-market instrument would be clearly advisable.

5. *Comparative levels of reserve coefficients.* Closing the large gap in the reserve coverage of time deposits (Point 3) is a worthwhile goal in itself. To close that deficiency in the manner described in Point 3 (by restoring uniform reservability to all time deposits and retaining the existing pair of reserve coefficients for transaction and time deposits) however, would not address the question of whether 12 percent and 3 percent constitute the most appropriate relative levels. The findings of the present study stress the following points. Removal of interest-rate ceilings and the lively competition among depositories have sharply reduced the differences among the several classes of deposit. Almost four-fifths of all deposits at commercial banks bear interest, and at other depository institutions the proportion is greater. Of equal importance, one-half of bank deposit balances are endowed with check-writing privileges, and all accounts now provide the holder a high degree of liquidity and transferability. Consequently, the demand privilege is no longer confined to demand (and other transaction) accounts. Otherwise expressed, the transaction deposits at a given moment do not accurately define "balances immediately available for making payments."

• Under these conditions, the 9 percentage-point differential between the reserve requirement ratio on transaction deposits and that on time deposits appears inconsistent with the perception that the account-holder has of the fairly similar properties of the respective accounts. It also seems to exaggerate the difference in risk incurred by the issuing bank in offering transaction accounts. If these points are correct, the present spread in ratios reinforces other incentives of the two parties to engage in deposit-sweeping and similar cash management schemes that add to the general churning-about of funds. The author therefore recommends a revision in the reserve requirement ratios that would either substantially narrow the difference between the two, or eliminate it entirely by moving eventually to a single ratio if that proved feasible.

• The Fed possesses the necessary data for calculating what alternative pairs of reserve ratios would produce a total reserve stock approximately equal to the level that would result *after* removing the exemptions described in Point 3. In the process, the beneficial effects as well as any negative effects of the change proposed here should be carefully verified and the timing of its adoption judiciously chosen.

In the course of exploring some consequences that may arise if the payments system becomes *fully* automated, Tobin arrives at a proposed basis for required reserves that essentially resembles what is recommended here. He would base required reserves on total bank assets, including overdraft advances outstanding, minus capital liabilities and assets representing subordinated debt. Since

$$\text{Assets} - \text{Capital} = \text{Liabilities}$$

Tobin's plan would be roughly equivalent to requiring reserves on all deposit liabilities, as recommended in Point 3 above.[39] He does not specify the reserve ratios, but the plausible inference from his paper is that they would not be far apart.

6. *Non-deposit sources of funds.* Several of the above paragraphs propose ways of improving the functioning of the required reserve instrument, as presently conceived within the general framework of monetary policy. While some aspects of the financial innovations and discovered loopholes that are raising problems for monetary control can be solved through adapting the reserve requirements, this may not be efficacious for all of them. As conceived in the Federal Reserve Act, the reserve requirements were to apply to the deposit liabilities that were borrowed from non-bank depositors and then lent by the banking system to non-bank enterprises. The commercial banks were the predominant intermediary between real agents, and the Fed regulations excluded interbank balances and items in process of collection from the calculation of deposits requiring reserves. This all seemed consistent in a financial setting in which banks' borrowing rates were fairly stable, maturities were adhered to, "managed" liabilities played a smaller role, and lending was mostly at fixed rates. It is widely recognized that market developments have greatly increased the number and types of financial instruments and institutions, and a larger portion of bank transactions is now with other domestic and foreign banks and other financial organisms.

• It is recommended that the Fed and other authorities, in the interest of vigilant ongoing policy review, analyze the reasons for and effects of several financial practices that are presently permitted, and reappraise the Fed's policy position regarding them. The list should include, but not necessarily be limited to:

a. Cash-management sweeping;
b. Reserve-requirement status of federal fund transactions, including the "continuing contract" type;

c. Repurchase and matched-transaction agreements;
d. Various off-balance-sheet activities, including interest-rate options, note issuance facilities, guarantees, options, and forward rate agreements; and
e. Practice of third-party transfers from money market mutual fund accounts.

7. *Discretion, management, and automaticity.* All three qualities mentioned in this caption are employed in some degree and some situations in the conduct of Federal Reserve monetary policy. When properly adjusted and applied, the reserve instrument operates in automatic fashion to call for a rise or a reduction in the stock of reserves in response to movements in reservable deposit (and other) liabilities. The other control instruments can, under these conditions, be used flexibly and discretely to facilitate market functioning and deal with significant deviations and exogenous shocks.

The Fed does indeed act with discretion, especially in the sense of defining the projected path of a given targeted variable as a range or cone, rather than a straight line. Moreover, it has not felt obliged to produce a rigid month-to-month rate of monetary growth, and has revised a range when new information made that seem clearly advisable, in consideration of all objectives. In short, the "rules" decided by the FOMC for open-market intervention are not too narrowly defined, and are interpreted in practice with judgment.

It must be recognized that the Fed monetary control system, taken as a whole, embodies a great deal of discretionary management. Except for the automatic response of required reserves, all control instruments are operated in timing, type, and volume upon the deliberate judgment or initiative of the Board and FOMC. Borrowing at the discount window by an individual bank is at that institution's initiative, but total borrowing by the banking system is one of the principal targets controlled. For the three months between FOMC meetings, open-market operations are performed at a high rate of daily activity on the basis of information, projections, and conjecture about how much and whether banking system reserves should temporarily be raised or lowered. Taken together, these measures constitute a highly *managed* monetary control policy.

On the whole—and particularly during the past four years—the results have been a generally satisfactory central bank policy, especially given the lack of a suitable governmental fiscal policy. Yet one would like to see the results of further research on the effects of this active degree of money-market management. That research should take into account, among other elements, the fact that the U.S. money and capital markets are highly articulated and adjustable, and they have access to, and from, the instrumentalities and resources in international markets. Apart from times of large-scale exogeneous shocks, could the private markets perhaps adjust satisfactorily with a somewhat lower degree of day-to-day Fed intervention? Might an accommodative readiness or zeal by the central bank result in facilitating to some extent the growth of the same financial innovations that are causing concern to monetary authorities?

Notes

1. The reserves side of this relationship can be defined in terms of total reserves, required reserves (i.e., legally mandated), or the borrowed and non-borrowed portions of total reserves. The Fed regularly projects and monitors all of these measures of the banks' reserves stock; but its focus operationally is on borrowed and non-borrowed reserves.

2. Mayer *et al.,* Chapter 22; Kaufman, pp. 211–215; Board of Governors, pp. 27, 57.

3. Robert V. Roosa, *Federal Reserve Operations in the Money and Government Securities Markets,* Federal Reserve Bank of New York, 1956. This book has been a model of perception and exposition to later examinations of Fed monetary action. The term "dynamic" was a judicious choice, rather than a cruder antonym to "defensive," such as "aggressive."

4. E.g., B. Friedman; Morris; Brainard and Perry, pp. 266–272; Tobin (1985); Bryant, pp. 81–89.

5. In the Fed money-stock tables for that month, "other checkable" deposits at commercial banks accounted for 21 percent of M1 and those at thrifts for 10 percent. For thrifts, the figures on other checkable deposits include a small, unspecified amount of demand deposits in addition to NOW and ATS.

6. E.g., see Simpson's paper and the discussion of it by Blinder, Duesenberry, and Hall in Brainard and Perry, pp. 249–272; and the presentation by Kasriel of two variants of the consequences.

7. See p. xxi. According to Simpson's findings, the downward pressure on elasticity would be greater if the rate paid on checkable deposits were a variable rather than a fixed one. In January 1986, rate ceilings were removed from all NOW accounts, and they are free to vary.

8. Hadjimichalakis, Chapters 6 and 7.

9. "There is a cost to a bank of managing its portfolio in such a way as to be able to honor uncertain deposit withdrawals on demand. This cost will be reflected in a lower rate . . . than rates paid on nontransactions assets." Kasriel, p. 10. Although the risk posed in standing ready to honor withdrawals on sight undoubtedly has been an important factor in the treatment accorded demand deposits (on both interest and reserve ratios) in the past, this uncertainty regarding transfers now increasingly attaches to all accounts.

10. Cf. Wenninger and Radecki.

11. Regulation D defined reservable demand deposits as gross demand deposits, minus cash items in process of collection and demand balances due from domestic banks. The reserve ratios were graduated by deposit-size intervals, but there was no zero-reserve bracket.

12. See Note 19 to Chapter 2.

13. See Meek (1985), pp. 28–35.

14. Brainard and Perry, pp. 266–267.

15. Table 2.3. The corresponding figures for all depository institutions are shown in Table 2.4.

16. Board of Governors, pp. 66 and 70; Pierce, p. 37.

17. Board of Governors, p. 69. See also Laurent, p. 18ff; Tobin (1986).

18. We have shown in Chapter 2 that these accounts often serve as feeder accounts for lateral transfer to checkable accounts, through direct or informal linkages.

19. See Wallich (1984), pp. 1–10.

20. Cf. Pierce, pp. 43–44. In this paragraph and the preceding example, I am analyzing the implications for open-market operations created by (a) the major exemptions and (b) overall reduction in required reserves produced by the MCA. While Pierce is mainly concerned with how to model a completely deregulated financial system in which he assumes that reserve requirements would be fully absent, his analysis is comparable with mine.

21. Although the subject of required reserve levels is normally and correctly considered from the standpoint of its macroeconomic role as an instrument of national monetary policy, it is worth noting that some individual banks appear to find that present required levels are not sufficient for their needs. Commenting on the continued rise in the average level of excess reserves since 1980, Anne-Marie Meulendyke and Sandra Krieger said, "Lower requirements left banks with less maneuvering room to assure a positive balance in their reserve account each night, and led some banks to hold a greater reserve cushion relative to requirements." *Quarterly Review,* Federal Reserve Bank of New York, Spring 1986, p. 43; also pp. 24–26. Other factors may also be contributing to raise excess reserve holdings.

22. The only provision in the MCA about the open-market activity was language empowering the Fed to purchase and sell obligations of, or fully guaranteed by, a foreign government. This authority has not so far been utilized for monetary control purposes. It would permit the Fed to convert some foreign-currency balances into earning assets.

23. The F.R. Banks also own some Federal agency obligations, which, in December 1986 were about 5 percent as large as the direct Treasury obligations held. Although eligible for use in market operations, their employment currently is irregular and small. Figures in the text and tables in this paper refer only to the direct government securities.

24. These terms, as here defined, are not part of common market terminology, but they appear useful in gaining an understanding of the nature and dimensions of monetary control operations. The same is true of the computed "turnover rates" in Table 3.5 which, to the author's knowledge, is a velocity measurement not generally used in a central-bank context.

25. See Board of Governors (1984), pp. 39–43; Young, pp. 61–66. Meek (1982) and (1985), currently the most exhaustive narrator about open-market operating techniques since Roosa, provides a somewhat fuller but more conditional rationale for the choice of technique, largely on a case basis.

26. Meek (1982), pp. 117–18. Among other cautions of this kind, he says that the trading desk sometimes buys Treasury coupon securities also, "when a sustained reserve need is projected and market availability is great enough to limit the price effects of buying."

27. Meek (1985), p. 41.

28. In addition to the terms "defensive" and "dynamic," Federal Reserve parlance also employs the terms "orderly-market oriented" and "policy oriented" in a roughly comparable sense: i.e., to connote a difference in motivation of given Fed actions in a contrasting, rather than antonymous, manner.

29. Young, p. 61.

30. "Each day the manager must decide whether to buy or sell outright, or to do so with a string attached. . . . Daily decisions seek to weave a pattern which is consistent with the inter-meeting objectives" of the FOMC. Meek (1982), p. 116.

31. Debits to demand deposits are shown as the average of monthly data, in trillions; FOMC transactions are from Table 3.5, in billions; required reserves are from F.R. *Bulletin,* monthly averages, in billions. The reader is reminded that the use of the ratio (logarithmic) scale has the advantage that a constant slope of a curve reflects a constant growth rate; parallelism between two curves shows equality in their growth rates. The *level* of the curve of demand-deposit debits should be disregarded, recognizing that it is plotted in trillions and the other two in billions.

32. Wallich (1984), and Solomon.

33. During the first half of the 1980s, the *volume* of intervention appears not to have depended materially upon whether the Fed's intermediate target was un-borrowed or borrowed reserves; but this matter would need further research and, in any case, lies outside the scope of this paper.

34. "It is ironic that the system should be tailored for M1 control just when the point of targeting M1 is widely and seriously doubted. . . ." Tobin (1985), p. 608. See also Board of Governors, pp. 33 and 69.

35. Although changes occurred in the *number* of dealers in the Fed's reporting panel, it is believed that market coverage is comparable over the years mentioned. The data on outright transactions by FOMC include redemptions, while the dealers' reports do not. This discrepancy is small, and exaggerates only slightly the FOMC market share.

36. Merris and Wood, p. 72.

37. Corrigan (1985–1986), pp. 1–5. Although his article is partly addressed to bank supervision and security aspects, Corrigan also touches on monetary control implications. He cites that it is "not uncommon" for computerized payments processed in New York by the F.R. Bank and the clearing house to exceed $1 trillion in one day.

38. Bingham terms this process "marketisation." This and the following paragraph draw especially on his authoritative treatment of the modification of central bank policy measures in Europe and Japan in response to the changed practices and structures. Bingham, pp. 97–158. See also Study Group, pp. 174–186 and 245–254. For a perceptive analysis of monetary policy in key European countries through 1972, see Hodgman (1974).

39. Tobin's paper appears in a book published and received after this manuscript was drafted. His proposed reserve base explicitly "in effect extends reserve requirements to . . . time deposits and CDs," saying that these "will be even more easily transferable" under a fully automated system than now. See James Tobin (1986), p. 195.

Glossary

Given below are summary definitions of terms appearing in this book, as well as certain abbreviations. In many cases, the term is also defined in the pertinent portion of the text. Since some of these terms are exhaustively defined by statute or Federal Reserve regulations, the aim here is to provide brief working explanations.

Bank Deposit Terminology

Demand deposit (= checking account). A bank account payable to the depositor on demand and transferable by him to others by drawing a check. By law, no interest is paid.

Savings deposit. An interest-bearing account in a bank or thrift institution on which additions or withdrawals made by the depositor are recorded in a passbook or monthly statement. No checks may be drawn.

Time deposit.
  a. In general, an interest-bearing deposit account or certificate payable to the depositor only on a specified date or after a specified period. The term "time deposits" is sometimes used to include also savings accounts.
  b. *Nonpersonal time deposit* is a statutory term referring to any time account or certificate of which the holder is not a natural person or charitable organization.
  c. *Certificate of deposit (CD)* is a time deposit issued for a specific principal amount and a fixed maturity. The large-denomination CD ($100,000 or larger) can be sold by the holder through dealers, some of whom make a secondary market in CDs. The small-denomination CD is not negotiable but may be redeemed from the issuing bank before maturity, subject to an interest penalty.

ATS account (Automatic transfer service). An interest-bearing account from which funds are shifted to the same depositor's checking account when the latter reaches a certain minimum balance.

NOW account (Negotiable order of withdrawal). Interest-bearing account on which unlimited number of checks can be drawn. May be offered by a bank or thrift institution, but to individuals or non-profit organizations only.

Other checkable deposits. A term embracing the NOW and ATS accounts at commercial banks and thrift institutions, as well as credit union "share draft" balances.

MMDA (Money market deposit account). An interest-bearing bank deposit account, classified within the time and savings category, with no specified maturity (but institutions must announce the right to require at least 7 days' notice prior to withdrawal) and with no restrictions on depositor eligibility. Banks are authorized to permit up to 6 transfers per month, no more than 3 of which may be drafts, in addition to unlimited withdrawals by mail, messenger, or in person.

Transaction deposits. A term created by statute to apply to depository institutions' accounts that do not specify a limit on the number of third-party transfers. At present, the group comprises demand deposits and other checkable deposits (q.v.).

Central Bank Structure and Terminology

Central bank. The central bank of any nation is that officially designated financial institution established to influence the volume and terms of money and credit, in the interest of assuring that their availability is neither inadequate nor excessive to the economy's ability to grow in accordance with its potential and with reasonable price stability. A central bank usually is the issuer of part or all of the national currency; supervises the banking system; and influences, through its monetary policy actions, the level of interest rates and volume of monetary resources in financial markets. It constitutes the lender of last resort.

Federal Reserve System (FRS). The name designated by Congress, in the Federal Reserve Act of 1913, for the central bank of the United States. It is an institution of complex structure, whose main functional components are the Board of Governors; the Federal Open Market Committee; and the twelve regional Federal Reserve Banks. Although established by statute and obligated by certain Congressional reporting requirements, it is generally recognized as being "independent within the government."

Federal Reserve Board (The Board, or FRB). The Board, consisting of seven members appointed by the President and confirmed by the Senate, is a powerful body whose main responsibility is in formulating the nation's monetary policy. It also has supervisory responsibilities over various private-sector financial institutions, the operations of the Federal Reserve Banks, and the functioning of the country's payment system. FRB members serve a 14-year term; the Chairman and Vice Chairman are appointed by the President, from FRB members, for a 4-year term.

Federal Open Market Committee (FOMC). Through purchases or sales of Treasury or Federal agency securities in the securities market, the Federal Reserve authorities increase or reduce the monetary resources available to the depository institutions. The FOMC decides on the general nature and objectives to be achieved by this market intervention, which is executed on a day-to-day basis by the Trading Desk at the New York Federal Reserve Bank. FOMC is composed of the seven Board members and five Reserve Bank presidents.

Federal Reserve Banks. The U.S. is divided into twelve Federal Reserve districts. In a major city in each district is a Reserve Bank, which carries out most of the operating transactions between the Federal Reserve System and the private-sector financial institutions and the public.

Member bank. Commercial banks that are Federally chartered are obliged to be "members of the Federal Reserve System"; state-chartered banks may also apply for membership. A member owns capital stock in the Reserve Bank of its District, in an amount based on the member's capitalization. Members are obliged to comply with FRB reporting instructions and to conform to the reserve requirements of the Board; they also have access to borrow from their respective Reserve Banks and to purchase the Fed's check-clearing and other services. Legislation in 1980 extended the rights and obligations of the preceding sentence to all depository institutions (q.v.). In 1985, banks with 71 percent of all commercial bank deposits held membership status.

Depository institutions. In general, the term refers to those financial institutions that accept deposits and make loans of one or more types. The phrase "banks and thrift institutions" is used here in the same sense. For statistical purposes, this book, like the Federal Reserve Board, adopts the definition of depositories in the Depository Institutions Deregulation and Monetary Control Act of 1980—as covering commercial banks, savings banks, savings and loan associations, credit unions, and U.S. agencies or branches of foreign banks.

Discount rate. The interest rate at which eligible depositories may obtain short-term loans from the Reserve Banks. Its level affects, and is strongly affected by, the levels of other major money-market rates.

Discount window. This homey, understated expression is the shorthand term for a Reserve Bank's department for lending to eligible depository institutions. These short-term loans are usually advances made to the borrowing bank on its note, secured by satisfactory collateral.

Federal funds. Immediately available reserve balances that one depository institution lends another, usually for an overnight period.

Open-market operations. This expression refers to purchase or sale transactions in the government securities market by the central bank authorities for the purpose of augmenting or reducing the amount of monetary resources available to depository institutions. In the United States, this intervention is carried out by the Trading Desk of the Federal Open Market Committee (q.v.). The open-market operations are accorded top responsibility among the Fed's instruments of monetary control and are conducted in high volume (see Chapter 3, Sec. 4). An open-market transaction can be an "outright transaction"—i.e., a straight purchase or sale. Preponderantly, however, operations by FOMC are by (a) "repurchase agreements," Fed purchases of a given amount of securities for immediate delivery embodying an agreement to sell that amount back to the same party within a specified, very short period and at a specified interest rate or price; or by (b) "matched sale-purchase transactions," the reverse of a repurchase agreement.

Required reserves. The dollar volume of money which a depository institution is obliged to hold, in its own vaults or on deposit at its Reserve Bank, in a given period. For macroeconomic purposes, the significant amount is the aggregate amount of required reserves of all depositories combined.

Reservable deposits (= deposits subject to reserve requirements). Under banking law, not all types of bank deposits are subject to the obligation to set aside reserves. Since 1980, deposits classified as time or savings accounts owned by individuals and households are exempt; and the only domestic deposits that bear required reserves are transaction accounts (demand and other checkable accounts, q.v.) and nonpersonal time deposits of less than 18 months.

Reserve requirements. Within a range established by law, the Federal Reserve Board fixes the percentage ratio of required reserves that banks and other depositories must maintain, in their own vaults or at their Reserve Banks, against each type of reservable deposit. In recent years, these percentage ratios or coefficients have been as follows: for transaction deposits, 12%; for nonpersonal time and savings deposits of less than 18 months, 3%; for net liabilities to foreign banking offices, 3%. (See the respective deposit definitions; and Required Reserves).

Depository Institutions Deregulation and Monetary Control Act of 1980 (MCA). This lengthy legislation dealt with numerous aspects of the status, powers, and activities of depository institutions. Its provisions pertinent to this book are that the MCA provided for the elimination of governmental authority to limit the rates of interest payable on deposits (Chap. 1); lowered the reserve requirements applicable to member banks on some types of deposit; exempted other deposit types from reserve requirements; and simultaneously extended the restructured rates to all depository institutions; accorded to the enlarged group the right to buy the Fed's financial services and borrow at the discount window (Chap. 2).

Bibliography

Axilrod, Stephen H., "U.S. Monetary Policy in Recent Years: An Overview." *Federal Reserve Bulletin*, January 1985, pp. 14–24.

Bingham, T.R.G., *Banking and Monetary Policy*. Paris, Organization for Economic Cooperation and Development, 1985.

Blinder, Alan S., in *Brookings Papers on Economic Activity*, 1:1984, William C. Brainard and George L. Perry, eds., pp. 266–70. Washington, Brookings Institution, 1984.

Board of Governors, *The Federal Reserve System: Purposes and Functions*. Washington, Board of Governors of the Federal Reserve System, 1984.

Brainard, William C., and Perry, George L., eds., *Brookings Papers on Economic Activity*, 1:1984. Washington, Brookings Institution, 1984.

Bryant, Ralph C., *Controlling Money: The Federal Reserve and its Critics*. Washington, Brookings Institution, 1983.

Cargill, Thomas F., and Garcia, Gillian G., *Financial Deregulation and Monetary Control: Historical Perspective and Impact of the 1980 Act*. Stanford, Hoover Institution Press, 1982.

Corrigan, E. Gerald, "Bank Supervision in a Changing Environment." *Quarterly Review*, Federal Reserve Bank of New York, Winter 1985–86, pp. 1–5.

————, "Financial Market Structure: A Longer View," in *Seventy-second Annual Report* (for 1986), Federal Reserve Bank of New York, 1987.

Crane, Dwight B., *The Effects of Banking Deregulation*. Washington, Association of Reserve City Bankers, 1983.

Duesenberry, James S., "The Political Economy of Central Banking in the United States," in Donald R. Hodgman, ed., *The Political Economy of Monetary Policy: National and International Aspects*. Boston, Federal Reserve Bank of Boston, 1983.

Eguchi, H., and Suzuki, Y., eds. *Monetary Policy in Our Times*. Cambridge (Mass.), MIT Press, 1985.

Federal Reserve Bank of Chicago, *Leveling the Playing Field: A Review of the DIDMCA of 1980 and the Garn-St. Germain Act of 1982*. Chicago, 1983.

Friedman, Benjamin M., "Time to Re-examine the Monetary Targets Framework." *New England Economic Review*, Federal Reserve Bank of Boston, March/April 1982.

Hadjimichalakis, Michael G., *The Federal Reserve, Money, and Interest Rates*. New York, Praeger Publishers, 1984.

Henderson, John B., *Money and Near-Monies: A Primer.* (Committee Print 98-6, prepared for the House Committee on Banking, Finance, and Urban Affairs.) Washington, U.S. Government Printing Office, 1983.

Hodgman, Donald R., *National Monetary Policies and International Monetary Cooperation.* Boston, Little, Brown and Company, 1974.

Kanatas, George, and Greenbaum, Stuart I., "Bank Reserve Requirements and Monetary Aggregates." *Journal of Banking and Finance,* 6:1982, pp. 507–20.

Kasriel, Paul L., "Is Deposit Rate Deregulation an Rx for M1?" *Economic Perspectives,* Federal Reserve Bank of Chicago, September/October, 1985, pp. 6–15.

Kaufman, George G., *Money, the Financial System, and the Economy.* Chicago, Rand McNally & Co., 1973.

Kettl, Donald F., *Leadership at the Fed.* New Haven, Yale University Press, 1986.

Klein, Michael A., "Monetary-Control Implications of the Monetary Control Act." *Economic Review,* Federal Reserve Bank of San Francisco, Winter 1981, pp. 6–21.

Laurent, Robert D., "Universal Reserve Requirements and Monetary Control." *Economic Perspectives,* Federal Reserve Bank of Chicago, September/October 1985.

Mayer, Thomas, *Monetary Policy in the United States.* New York, Random House, 1968.

Mayer, Thomas; Duesenberry, James S.; and Aliber, Robert Z., *Money, Banking, and the Economy.* New York, W.W. Norton & Co., 1981.

Meek, Paul, *U.S. Monetary Policy and Financial Markets.* New York, Federal Reserve Bank of New York, 1982.

———— , *Open Market Operations.* New York, Federal Reserve Bank of New York, 1985.

Melton, William C., *Inside the Fed: Making Monetary Policy.* Homewood, Illinois, Dow Jones–Irwin, 1985.

Merris, Randall C., and Wood, John, "A Deregulated Re-run: Banking in the Eighties." *Economic Perspectives,* Federal Reserve Bank of Chicago, September/October 1985, pp. 69–78.

Minsky, Hyman P., "Money and the Lender of Last Resort." *Challenge,* March-April 1985, pp. 12–18.

Morris, Frank E., "Do the Monetary Aggregates Have a Future as Targets of Federal Reserve Policy?" *New England Economic Review,* Federal Reserve Bank of Boston, March/April 1982.

Pierce, James L., "Some Public Policy Issues Raised by the Deregulation of Financial Institutions." *Contemporary Policy Issues,* No. 2, January 1983, pp. 33–48.

President's Commission on Financial Structure and Regulation, *Report.* (Also known as the Hunt Report.) Washington, U.S. Government Printing Office, 1972.

Public Law 96–221, 96th Congress (Depository Institutions Deregulation and Monetary Control Act of 1980). *U.S.C.S.* May 1980, pp. 2338–99.

Roosa, Robert V., *Federal Reserve Operations in the Money and Government Securities Markets.* New York, Federal Reserve Bank of New York, 1956.

Samuelson, Paul A., *Economics* (11th ed.). New York, McGraw-Hill Book Co., 1980.

Sayers, R.S., *Central Banking after Bagehot.* London, Greenwood Press, new ed., 1982.

Simpson, Thomas D., "Changes in the Financial System: Implications for Monetary Policy." *Brookings Papers on Economic Activity,* 1:1984, pp. 249 ff.

Solomon, Anthony M., "Some Problems and Prospects for Monetary Policy in 1985." *Quarterly Review,* Federal Reserve Bank of New York, Winter 1984–85, pp. 1–6.

Sternlight, Peter D., and Levin, Fred J., "Open-market operations," in *Encyclopedia of Economics,* Douglas Greenwald, ed. New York, McGraw-Hill Book Company, 1982, pp. 711–715.

Study Group established by the central banks of the Group of Ten Countries, *Recent Innovations in International Banking.* Basle, Bank for International Settlements, 1986.

Tobin, James, prepared *Comment* on "On Consequences and Criticisms of Monetary Targeting." *Journal of Money, Credit, and Banking,* vol. 17, No. 4 (November 1985, Part 2).

————, "Monetary Control in a Brave New World." In Colin Lawrence and Robert P. Shay, eds., *Technological Innovation, Regulation, and the Monetary Economy,* pp. 190–195, 207–208. Cambridge (Mass.), Ballinger Publishing Company, 1986.

U.S. Congress. Senate. Committee on Banking, Housing, and Urban Affairs, 96th Congress, 2nd session. *Federal Reserve Requirements.* Hearings on S. 353 and proposed amendments, S. 85, and H.R. 7 (to facilitate the implementation of monetary policy and to promote competitive equality among depository institutions), Feb. 4 and 5, 1980.

Wallich, Henry C., "Recent Techniques of Monetary Policy." *Economic Review,* Federal Reserve Bank of Kansas City, May 1984.

————, "Whither American Banking Reform." *Challenge,* September-October 1985, pp. 43–46.

Wenninger, John, and Radecki, Lawrence J., "The Monetary Aggregates in 1985." *Quarterly Review,* Federal Reserve Bank of New York, Winter 1985–86, pp. 6–10.

Wojnilower, Albert M., "The Central Role of Credit Crunches in Recent Financial History." *Brookings Papers on Economic Activity,* 2:1980, pp. 277–339. Washington, Brookings Institution, 1981.

Young, Ralph A., *Instruments of Monetary Policy in the United States: The Role of the Federal Reserve System.* Washington, International Monetary Fund, 1973.

Index